WORKING WITH MARGINALISED GROUPS

WORKING WITH MARGINALISED GROUPS

FROM POLICY TO PRACTICE

EDITED BY ANYA AHMED
AND MICHAELA ROGERS

First published 2016 by
PALGRAVE

Palgrave in the UK is an imprint of Macmillan Publishers Limited,
registered in England, company number 785998, of 4 Crinan Street,
London, N1 9XW.

Palgrave® and Macmillan® are registered trademarks in the United States,
the United Kingdom, Europe and other countries.

ISBN 978–1–137–55956–2 paperback

This book is printed on paper suitable for recycling and made from fully
managed and sustained forest sources. Logging, pulping and manufacturing
processes are expected to conform to the environmental regulations of the
country of origin.

A catalogue record for this book is available from the British Library.

A catalog record for this book is available from the Library of Congress.

Printed and bound in the UK by The Lavenham Press Ltd, Suffolk.

CONTENTS

Notes on the Contributors   ix

Acknowledgements   xv

Introduction   **1**
Anya Ahmed and Michaela Rogers

1 Diversity and exclusion in context   **6**
Anya Ahmed and Michaela Rogers

Introduction   6
Theoretical and conceptual frameworks   7
The practice framework   11
The policy framework   13
The legislative framework   14
Conclusion   18
Recommended reading   18
Relevant web links   18
References   19

**2 Identity, difference and the meaning of 'culture' in health
and social care practice**   **21**
Julie Morton and Steve Myers

Introduction   21
Concepts of difference, identity and 'culture'   22
Culture and cultural competence   25
Consequences for practice   26
Alternative ways of viewing difference for practitioners   27
Working with difference in health and social care case studies   29
Interrogating the practitioner's assessment   30
Problematising this assessment   30
Consequences   30
Alternative ways of understanding   30
Interrogating the practitioner's assessment   31
Problematising the assessment   32
Consequences   32
Alternative ways of understanding   32
Key messages for health and social care practice   33
Conclusion   34

Recommended reading   34
Relevant web links   35
References   35

**3 Young people as carers and young users of
mental health services: from policy to practice**   **37**
Sue McAndrew and Tony Warne

Introduction   37
Young people and mental health problems   38
Young carers   39
Synopsis of the adult service user and carer movement   40
Extending the movement to young people   40
The nuances of involving young people in education, practice
    and research   42
Concerns and possible (im)practicalities   44
Conclusion   47
Recommended reading   48
Relevant web links   48
References   48

**4 Marginalised children and young people with
autism spectrum disorders**   **52**
Andrea Brammer, Rob Kennedy and Frances Binns

Introduction   52
The global context   53
Associated comorbidities of ASD and medical interventions   54
Economic impact and resources   55
Equality in accessing healthcare   55
Barriers to health and diagnostic treatment   56
Reasonable adjustments   58
Reasonable adjustments to support equitable access to healthcare 59
Person Centred Needs Assessments (PCNA)   60
Transition to adult services   62
Conclusion   63
Recommended reading   64
Relevant web links   64
References   64

5 Understanding the social exclusion of Roma   **70**
Lisa Scullion and Philip Brown

Introduction   70
Defining Roma   71
The social exclusion of Roma: a 'European issue'   72
Roma in the UK   77

Conclusion   81
Recommended reading   81
Relevant web links   82
References   82

6 Trans and gender diversity: messages for policy
** and practice   86**
  Michaela Rogers

Introduction   86
Theoretical and conceptual frameworks   87
A marginalised population?   91
Citizenship and trans communities   92
The policy framework   94
Key issues for practice: barriers and challenges in practice contexts   96
Messages for health and social care providers   99
Conclusion   100
Recommended reading   101
Relevant web links   101
References   101

7 Deafness and social exclusion   105
  Naomi Sharples and Will Hough

Introduction   105
Historical context   105
Models that help understand d/Deafness   107
Legislation and policy   109
Deaf people's access to healthcare   110
Deaf people's access to psychiatric services   111
Communication   113
Communication strategies   114
Deaf people and employment   116
Deaf children's education: the present context   116
Conclusion   117
Recommended reading   118
Relevant web links   118
References   118

8 Dementia, diverse communities and access to services 120
  Anya Ahmed, Ubah Egal and Shahid Mohammed

Introduction   120
Understanding race, culture and ethnicity   121
Socio-demographic processes behind ageing and migration in the UK   122
Understanding dementia   123
The policy and practice context   125

Dementia and BME communities   126
Conclusion   130
Recommended reading   131
Relevant web links   131
References   132

**9 Older women's experiences of domestic violence
  and abuse   134**
Michaela Rogers

Introduction   134
Domestic abuse and an ageing population   135
Elder abuse or domestic violence?   135
Challenges in measuring prevalence and analysing experience 137
Dynamics of abuse in later life   139
Barriers to help-seeking action   141
Enablers for help-seeking   143
DVA and the legal framework   144
Messages for health and social care providers   145
Conclusion   146
Recommended reading   147
Relevant web links   148
References   148

Conclusion   151
Anya Ahmed and Michaela Rogers

Index   155

NOTES ON THE CONTRIBUTORS

Dr Anya Ahmed
Anya is Senior Lecturer in Social Policy at the University of Salford, UK. Anya has a professional background in housing and an academic background in social policy and sociology. She has led numerous externally funded projects focusing on the experiences of less heard communities in the UK. She writes about ageing and older people, gender and different forms of mobility, including forced, economic and lifestyle migration. Anya is the lead for diversity and inclusion at the University of Salford's Institute for Dementia, and the lead for Housing and Homelessness in the Sustainable and Urban Studies Unit in the School of Nursing, Midwifery, Social Work and Social Sciences.

Frances Binns
Frances is the Consultant/Specialist Adviser Complex Needs: Autism and Learning Disabilities and Well Child Adviser UK at the Royal Manchester Children's Hospital. Frances has 38 years' experience in hospitals and other healthcare establishments working with children and young people from birth to 19 years old and their families, and in working to promote inclusivity, equality and diversity at a strategic and operational level. She has received the Nursing Times Awards and Unite the Union for Recognising Autism Management Programme and others, such as the NHS Hero for pushing boundaries. Frances developed the Royal Manchester Children's Hospital Recognising Autism Management Programme (RAMP) following service user/stakeholder participation. Frances's current work includes developing autism and learning disability friendly quality service improvements for children and young people and families with autism/learning disabilities and medical complexity when accessing hospital healthcare services. Frances is the autism champion model and promotes the model nationally and internationally.

Andrea Brammer
Andrea has worked as a diagnostic radiographer in the NHS since 1990, specialising as a paediatric radiographer in 2003 at the Royal Manchester Children's Hospital (RMCH). She helped to set up a radiographer-led micturating cystogram service in 2003, which resulted in improving the patient and families' experience while at the same time drastically reducing the waiting list for the examination. In 2005, Andrea became responsible for overseeing the departmental quality

assurance programme and ensuring compliance with the Ionising Radiation (Medical Exposure) Regulations 2000 (IRMER). In 2009, she moved with RMCH, merging with Booth Hall Children's Hospital into a purpose-built, state of the art hospital adjacent to Manchester Royal Infirmary: these hospitals comprise Central Manchester University Hospitals Foundation Trust. She became the Radiology Directorate Risk Manager and Clinical Effectiveness Lead in 2010, and completed an MSc in 'Leadership in Health and Social Care' in 2015 with a dissertation regarding improving access to healthcare for children with autism spectrum disorder. Andrea is also a committee member of the Association of Paediatric Radiographers and remains passionate about improving patient care, patient safety, quality and ensuring the voice of minority patients is heard and considered at all times.

Professor Philip Brown

Philip is Professor of Social Change and Director of the Sustainable Housing & Urban Studies Unit at the University of Salford, UK. He has led and delivered a wide range of projects for the private and public sector, charitable bodies and European Commission. These projects typically aim to identify and assess the impact of specific policy initiatives over a variety of issues, including social inclusion, migration, homelessness, fuel poverty, energy efficiency and regeneration. He has been involved in research examining Gypsy, Roma and Traveller inclusion since 2005. He was part of the team responsible for delivering the Roma SOURCE and Roma MATRIX projects which were co-funded with financial support from the Fundamental Rights and Citizenship Programme of the European Union. Philip is a Chartered Psychologist of the British Psychological Society and has written widely in a range of publications.

Ubah Egal

Ubah is the director of the Somali Cultural Centre in Camden, North London. Born in Uganda to a Somali Diplomat she spent her early years in Uganda, Kenya and Libya before settling in London in the early eighties. Ubah has a career portfolio spanning the arts and social justice with the common link between these otherwise disparate worlds being her passion for championing Somali culture. A trained and experienced social worker, Ubah is often called upon to bring her unique and specialist knowledge of working with her community to support some of the most vulnerable in the diaspora in education, judicial and social case work. In recent years Ubah has worked with leading academics to develop evidence-based research, including dementia in the Somali community. Ubah's work as a creative has included initiating programmes at The Roundhouse, contributing to BBC news documentaries and supporting playwrights at the National Theatre. When she is not working on community case work or creative projects she is developing her own writing.

Will Hough

Will is a registered mental health nurse. Since 1998 he has worked in the specialist field of Mental Health and Deafness, working as a staff nurse at the National Centre for Mental Health and Deafness in Manchester before moving to an independent provider, setting up as part of the Senior Nurse Team the first ever Medium Secure Service for Deaf People; this led to him specialising and completing his post graduate studies in the field of Assessment & Treatment of Sexual Offenders and creating specialised Sex Offender Treatment Programmes for Deaf People. He has worked alongside the Royal College of Psychiatry in producing standards of care for Deaf people within secure care and the roll out of the shared pathway through Deaf forensic services. He has written work around recovery models and the need to have a unilateral model across Deaf services. He is currently employed at the University of Salford, where he leads on the Deaf Mental Health Nurse Project.

Robert Kennedy

Robert is a lecturer in Children and Young People's Nursing. With over 25 years as a Children's Nurse, he has primarily worked with many children and young people who have Autism/Asperger's Syndrome in acute hospital and rehabilitative community settings. Many of these have experienced complicated treatment regimens following major trauma. He has experienced first-hand the inequalities in health that these individuals often experience, mainly unintentionally and due to a lack of forethought or insight/knowledge of their individualised health needs. He has very personal experiences of the breadth of the autistic spectrum as many male members of his family have Asperger's Syndrome. This has been his personal, key driver into wanting to fly the flag for Autism and change perceptions through the education of other healthcare staff and professions outside of the health arena. The key driver of his PhD work is the ultimate aim of having Autistic Spectrum Disorder recognised as 'every day' rather than the 'exception' that needs to be dealt with. Flying the flag for Autism will ultimately ensure that supportive strategies will become embedded into society, underpinned by central government and recognised as much as Dementia.

Dr Sue McAndrew

Sue is a Reader in Mental Health at the University of Salford. Sue has worked in mental health (MH) nursing since 1972. In 1992 she became a lecturer at the University of Leeds, where she worked for 17 years, during which time she continued to work 1 day per week in primary MH care. In 2009 Sue took up post as Research Fellow [MH] at University of Salford. Sue has published extensively and co-edited three books: *Sexual Health: Foundations for Practice*; *Using Patient Experience in Nurse Education*; and *Creative Approaches in Health and Social Care Education and Practice: Knowing Me, Understanding You*. Her research interests include childhood sexual abuse, self-harm, suicide, user/carer involve-ment, therapeutic engagement and preparation for the emotionality inherent in mental health nursing practice. Sue is associate editor for the *International Jour-nal of Mental Health Nursing* and currently chairs the Post Graduate Research, Innovation and Enterprise Ethics Panel.

Shahid Mohammed

Shahid worked within Learning, Skills and Community Development in the Public sector for over 24 years with organisations including the Training Enter-prise Council, Learning and Skills Council, Oldham Council and the British Council. In 2012 his mother's mental and physical health began to deteriorate, which led him to take early retirement from a long career in the Public sector, and he became a full-time carer. This led him to set out on a campaign to engage with the BME and South Asian community in Rochdale and he became the founder of BME Health and Wellbeing, raising awareness of dementia and providing help and advice to support services and other professionals. Shahid has been an important facilitator in promoting the awareness of Dementia within BME through his numerous TV and radio interviews, university lectures, peer support work, as a Police trainer and his strong partnerships with key organisations. Shahid is also a board member of Greater Manchester TellMAMA, a national project which records and measures anti-Muslim incidents in the United Kingdom. Separate to the dementia work, Shahid also actively cam-paigns on local issues – working with local councillors, council officers, the police and the local community in making the local area clean, green and safe; he is the founder of a local residents group 'KSERA'.

Julie Morton

Julie worked as an Approved Social Worker (ASW) in mental health for ten years in Greater Manchester. After becoming a lecturer, Julie taught modules on anti-oppressive practice and social work values. She developed an interest in how we might challenge conceptualisations of race and sexuality which both shape and limit the ways in which we think about and make sense of practice in health and social care. Julie continues to enjoy developing innovative ways of approaching the teaching of these subjects, and has presented at conferences on how ideas about race and sexuality are produced in social work and teaching. Her other interest is in research ethics and the meaning of ethics in institutions and professions.

Steve Myers

Steve is Director of Social Sciences at the University of Salford, UK. He is a regis-tered Social Worker and as such has worked in voluntary and statutory services, primarily with children and their families. He has researched and published about sex, violence and solution-focused practices, with a particular interest in responding to sexual violence. He teaches across a range of academic and pro-fessionally qualifying subject areas, including the Social Sciences, Social Work and Counselling, as well as providing training and CPD for professionals in the community. Steve is interested in the complexities of practice and in finding solutions that are simple without being simplistic.

Dr Michaela Rogers

Michaela is Lecturer in Social Work at the University of Salford, UK. She is a registered social worker and has a professional and academic background in social work and social care. Previously, her work in the statutory and voluntary sectors has involved working with different groups of vulnerable people (includ-ing young people, women and children escaping domestic abuse). Michaela's research has centred on the needs of vulnerable and marginalised communities (including trans people and people with mental health difficulties) in relation to social care and social work, and this extended to homelessness in her PhD research, which explored trans people's experiences of domestic abuse and the service response in terms of social care and housing-related support. Michaela is a member of the Sustainable Housing & Urban Studies Unit and the Children & Young People Research Group at the University of Salford.

Dr Lisa Scullion

Lisa is a Reader in Social Policy and Associate Director of the Sustainable Hous-ing & Urban Studies Unit at the University of Salford, UK. Her research focuses on the social welfare needs and experiences of a range of socially excluded communities, including Gypsies, Roma and Travellers, migrant populations and those subject to conditional welfare. Lisa was part of the team responsible for delivering the Roma SOURCE and Roma MATRIX projects, which were co-funded with financial support from the Fundamental Rights and Citizenship Programme of the European Union. She has also been involved in assessing the needs of Gypsies and Travellers within the UK since 2006.

Dr Naomi Sharples

Naomi worked as a qualified nurse and nurse manager at the National Centre for Mental Health and Deafness John Denmark Unit before becoming the lead for Deaf People's Access to Nurse Education project at the University of Salford, UK. Now working as Associate Dean at the University of Chester, UK, Naomi remains active and committed to improving student inclusion, health and well-being.

Professor Tony Warne

Tony is a Professor in Mental Health Care, and until recently, Head of the School of Nursing, Midwifery, Social Work & Social Sciences at the University of Salford, UK. The School holds one of the largest commissions of NHS programmes in the

North West and has a range of programmes in nursing, social work, social policy, midwifery, psychotherapy, sociology and criminology. Tony worked in NHS mental healthcare services from 1975, both as a practitioner and service manager. After leaving the NHS in 1995 he joined Manchester Metropolitan University, UK, gaining his PhD in 2000. In 2006, Tony was appointed Professor at the University of Salford, UK. The focus of his research interest is on inter-personal, intra-personal and extra-personal relationships, using a psychodynamic and managerialist analytical discourse. He has published extensively in these areas and is the co-editor and author of the books *Using Patient Experience in Nurse Education* and *Creative Approaches to Health and Social Care Education*. Tony is the Nurse Representative on the Council of Deans (Health) Executive Committee, which represents the 85 UK universities providing healthcare education. He is also a Non-Executive Director for the Wrightington, Wigan and Leigh NHS Trust, with a special interest in improving the quality and safety of patient care.

ACKNOWLEDGEMENTS

It's been a real pleasure co-editing this book with Michaela and I look forward to many more future collaborations. I'd also like to thank Nancy Smith for her involvement in developing the ideas for the book and for co-organising a Student Symposium in the School of Nursing, Midwifery, Social Work and Social Sciences at the University of Salford. This symposium brought together the diverse disciplines across the school and demonstrated our collective interest in and commitment to highlighting and addressing the marginalisation of the people and communities we research and work with. I'd also like to thank the contributors to the book for sharing their research and professional experiences here. Thank you to all those people – from a range of backgrounds, ages, ethnicities, cultures and contexts – who have participated in my research and shared experiences with me. Giving voice to experiences of discrimination and inequality and challenging structures which reinforce such experiences remains my primary motivation as a researcher. Finally, and on a personal note, I'd like to thank my family (Abdi Ahmed, Alison and Bazill Ahmed Barrett and all the Peacocks) for their love, support and encouragement. Most of all, and as ever, the biggest thanks go to my husband, Dan Peacock.

Dr Anya Ahmed, June 2016

First and foremost, I would like to say thank you to Anya, who gave me the opportunity to co-edit this book with her; it has been an eventful and exciting journey. I also would like to express gratitude to all the people who I have met throughout my career and who have shared their stories with me, but especially I remember those who have experienced life from a position that is marginalised. It is the people who have survived domestic violence and abuse, or hate crime, or discrimination purely because of how they dress or identify who have constantly reminded me of the reasons why I became involved in 'people work' in 1993. They have helped me to maintain my passion for social justice and the quest for fairness and equality. Lastly, but as always, I have to acknowledge the support and care that I receive from my family, as without them I could not do what I do. So, thank you Mick Ryan, Noah Ryan, Daisy Ryan, Marilyn Rogers and Andy Mortimer.

Dr Michaela Rogers, June 2016

We would like to thank Palgrave for publishing our book, and particularly Peter Hooper and Louise Summerling for their help and support throughout the process. We would also like to thank the anonymous reviewers for their helpful feedback, both at proposal stage and on submission of the draft manuscript.

INTRODUCTION

Anya Ahmed and Michaela Rogers

This book, aimed at health and social care students and practitioners, focuses on a range of practical topics which broadly – but not typically – fall within the remit of 'diversity'. We explore examples and experiences of 'diversity' and highlight a range of individuals and groups in UK society who experience exclusion or marginalisation differently. Written by experts, including academics and practitioners working in health and social care settings, this book contextualises diversity and exclusion using a range of theoretical perspectives. The idea for the book arose from conversations between us and with our colleagues in the School of Nursing, Midwifery, Social Work and Social Sciences at the University of Salford, UK. Although we are located in a school with people from a diversity of academic disciplines and professional backgrounds – and this is reflected by the different 'voices' in subsequent chapters – we share a common value base as well as a strong commitment to addressing inequality through learning, teaching and in how we prepare students for professional practice.

A key aim of the book, through its unique practice-based focus, is to encourage students as present and future practitioners to develop an enquiring mind in relation to diversity in UK society and to debunk myths about 'the others'. We aim to highlight cross-disciplinary themes while removing the idea of professional silos: an ongoing challenge within health and social care professional practice. We present 'real world' examples through the use of case studies, and the activities of each chapter are designed to help the reader apply theory and policy to practice. We also engage with current debates across the health and social care disciplines and highlight contemporary practice issues and challenges. The book captures theoretical, legislative, policy and practice issues across a range of groups, and each chapter includes topics for discussion for group work with students. The authors address diversity and exclusion along social divisions and how these cut across the life course (children and young people/adults) and considers how to practise in an inclusive way. The premise is that good practice is inclusive practice within the contexts of legislation, professional codes of practice and equality and diversity.

We focus on *examples* of 'marginalised groups' in the UK; these examples are included since they reflect the authors' academic and professional interests and expertise. Throughout the book we draw out the processes and outcomes of exclusion and also highlight the implications for practice, within relevant theoretical, legislative and policy contexts. However, we do acknowledge that the term 'marginalised groups' is problematic, mainly because it homogenises people who share certain characteristics and it also essentialises these characteristics. In other words, there is an inherent assumption that people who 'belong' to a certain 'group' in terms of gender, disability, sexuality, age or ethnicity, for example, have particular characteristics which define them. The term is also problematic as it suggests that the 'groups' are passive and this underplays the agency and resilience of individuals in society. We also acknowledge that some of the 'groups' under discussion (people from BME communities for example) are marginalised through social processes, and others (people with dementia) are excluded through disability. However, our focus is primarily on the processes and outcomes of exclusion and marginalisation and the theoretical, policy and practice implications.

The book is organised as follows: in the first chapter we outline the legal, policy and theoretical frameworks underpinning the following chapters. We highlight that although the UK is a relatively tolerant society and home to a diverse population, it is still characterised by inequality and exclusion. Significantly, clients of health and social care services are diverse in multiple ways since people occupy different 'categories' or social locations, as do individuals employed in health and social care professions. Importantly too, health and social care organisations are also diverse and are shaped by structural and ideological influences which can pose challenges to equitable service delivery. This first chapter explores the key concepts discussed throughout the book: diversity, discrimination, equality/diversity, intersectionality, social justice and exclusion/inclusion to frame the subsequent chapters. We argue that there is a need to problematise diversity and acknowledge the limitations of this concept in ensuring inclusive practice, maintaining that it should not be used to oversimplify complexity.

Diversity is presented as a conceptual tool to understand equality, and equality is considered as extending further than legal compliance to the Equality Act 2010. We argue that when discussing diversity, in addition to considering equality, debates on exclusion and inclusion also need to be taken into account. We posit that the debate needs to go beyond focusing on the characteristics of individuals and groups who are considered 'diverse' and should also take account of structural factors (societal and institutional) and the agency of professionals who have the power to exclude. In this way, we present exclusion as the processes and outcomes of diverse groups being treated less favourably. We argue that exclusion is conceptually useful when attempting to understand the experiences of people from diverse backgrounds, and establish the book's focus on the processes and outcomes of exclusion, considering how inclusive practice and anti-oppressive practice promote social justice.

In Chapter 2, Julie Morton and Steve Myers raise questions about identity, difference and the meaning of 'culture' in health and social care practice. Beginning with the premise that 'culture' is a key concept in discourses about difference and exclusion they question how 'culture' is conceptualised, used and performed in health and social care practice. Placed within the context of debates on multiculturalism and the relationship between culture and identity, Morton and Myers also problematise the idea of 'cultural competence' and highlight how approaches to teaching about culture in social work and health and social care often do not investigate norms, discourses and practices of dominant cultures. Instead, these are represented as neutral, and, as such, they question the ways in which the 'other' is constructed. Morton and Myers argue that despite benign intentions, practices can reinforce exclusion through the production of new understandings of 'difference' and/or 'need'. They suggest that reflexive practice approaches may be more helpful in understanding individuals in context and consequently provide more effective interventions.

The following chapters are organised according to different life course stages, beginning with young people in Chapters 3 and 4, while Chapters 5, 6 and 7 focus on adults. Chapters 8 and 9 focus on the experiences of older people. In Chapter 3, Sue McAndrew and Tony Warne consider how young people under 16 who are service users and carers are often marginalised and their contributions to research, education and practice overlooked. They highlight that the psychological well-being of young people who use mental health services and young people who have taken on a caring role is an important area of concern for a contemporary health and social care agenda. This is significant in two ways: there is an increased prevalence of mental illness among young people in general, and young carers in particular are vulnerable in terms of their mental health being compromised through the complex nature of taking on a caring role. McAndrew and Warne argue that there is a need to recognise the experiences of young service users and carers in order to promote better mental health, and that this is key to health and social care education, research and service delivery.

In Chapter 4, Andrea Brammer, Rob Kennedy and Frances Binns consider the marginalisation of children and young people with autism spectrum disorders. They highlight that the main challenges facing children and young people with autism spectrum disorders centre on social interactions and dealing with unfamiliar environments. A central focus of their discussion is that such challenges are particularly problematic when a child or young person requires healthcare intervention. Brammer, Kennedy and Binns place collaborative working between health and social care practitioners at the core of delivering appropriate services for children and young people with autism. They argue that there is a need to facilitate more understanding of the issues facing children and young people with autism spectrum disorders in order to inform practice and promote successful healthcare interventions.

In Chapter 5, Lisa Scullion and Phil Brown examine how Roma are socially excluded in the UK. They highlight that this population is one of the most socially excluded across contemporary Europe and identify a range of structural and cultural barriers impacting on health outcomes, educational attainment, employment, housing and social welfare. Scullion and Brown argue that although policy and practice are increasingly focused on addressing the exclusion of Roma at a European and national level, many of these initiatives do not offer long-term solutions. They identify how future approaches to Roma inclusion need to ensure the involvement of Roma in their development and implementation.

In Chapter 6, Michaela Rogers outlines the messages for policy and practice raised by trans and gender diversity, arguing that as trans people become increasingly visible in social life, the social problems that affect them also become more apparent. She premises that theoretical concepts such as heteronormativity, gender normativity and cisgenderism help to facilitate an understanding of trans people's social exclusion and marginalisation, but highlights how although policy and legislation recognises and protects some trans people, this is limited to those who identify within the confines of the gender binary. As such, there are multiple barriers for trans people accessing health and social care services and this raises questions of how practice can be inclusive.

In Chapter 7, Will Hough and Naomi Sharples consider deafness and social exclusion, highlighting that deaf people and people who are hard of hearing have experienced degrees of exclusion from the mainstream of society for millennia. They explain how such exclusion creates challenges and difficulties for individuals, their families and relationships, as well as adversely affecting educational attainment, employment and health and well-being. Hough and Sharples argue that equalising access to society's institutions is the most empowering of all acts that individuals, both deaf and hearing, can achieve because increased inclusion supports better education, employment and healthy lives.

In Chapter 8, Anya Ahmed, Ubah Egal and Shahid Mohammed address the issues facing BME communities in relation to experiences of dementia and accessing health and social care services. They begin by identifying dementia as the biggest health and social care challenge facing contemporary society, and explain that due to migration to the UK during the 1950s and 1960s, there is now an ageing BME population. They explain that although the number of people from BME backgrounds with dementia is rising, very little is known about their experiences and that this is problematic since their needs are not currently being met. Ahmed, Egal and Mohammed argue that as a result, people from these communities are not experiencing equitable health and social care, and are marginalised, which has consequences for the well-being of people living with dementia, their carers and family members.

In Chapter 9 Michaela Rogers identifies domestic violence and abuse (DVA) as a global problem and argues that developing appropriate responses is a challenge for health and social care services. She explains that DVA is entrenched and wide-reaching and that it assumes many different forms and has lasting impacts, with there being no type of 'perpetrator', nor a homogenous group of 'victims' or 'survivors'. Instead she unravels how DVA affects a diversity and multiplicity of people at different life-course junctures. Central to Rogers' discussion, is that older women have been neglected in DVA research and practice and as a result can be described as a 'hidden group', and that there are consequences to this in terms of understanding and acknowledging their experiences.

Finally, Ahmed and Rogers offer a conclusion where the key themes are summarised and framed within the context of good practice in health and social care being synonymous with inclusive practice.

1

DIVERSITY AND EXCLUSION IN CONTEXT

Anya Ahmed and Michaela Rogers

Chapter overview: **key messages**

- Although the UK is a relatively tolerant society with a diverse population, inequality and exclusion persist.
- It is necessary to problematise familiar concepts to understand their meaning and limitations.
- Focusing on the characteristics of diverse communities alone does not help us understand why they are 'excluded'.
- Inclusive models of practice in health and social care need to address structural or institutional factors, and also the agency of professionals who have the power to exclude.

Introduction

By focusing on the theoretical, legal and policy frameworks which underpin the debate about diversity and exclusion, this chapter serves as an introduction and as a backdrop to the book. Here we highlight that although the UK is a relatively tolerant society and home to a diverse population, it is still characterised by inequality and exclusion. For example, a substantially higher proportion of people who live in families with a disabled member live in poverty than households where no-one is disabled (DWP, 2014); people from minority ethnic communities are twice as likely to be unemployed than white people (DWP, 2014) and, in 2015, women who were working full-time earned just under 14 per cent less than men in full-time employment (ONS, 2015).

This chapter explores some key concepts that help to understand these claims and these help to frame the subsequent chapters in the book. The concepts are: equality and diversity, discrimination, exclusion/inclusion and intersectionality. We argue that there is a need to problematise some of these concepts (such as diversity and intersectionality) in order to understand how they are applied and have meaning, and also to be clear about their limitations. This is essential for the continuing development of inclusive practice models across health and social care organisations (for instance, anti-oppressive practice) which can often be criticised for oversimplifying complexity and homogenising difference. In this chapter, diversity is presented as a conceptual tool to understand equality, and equality is considered as extending further than legal compliance to the Equality Act 2010.

We argue that within a critical analysis of diversity and equality, debates on inclusion and exclusion should also be taken into account. Crucially, in terms of the development of health and social care, the debate about diversity needs to move beyond micro-level analysis (which focuses on the characteristics of individuals and groups considered to be 'diverse') to take account of structural factors (at the level of society and institutions). This discussion should include practitioners within health and social care, and also take account of the agency of professionals who have the power to exclude. In this way, we present exclusion as the processes and outcomes of when individuals and groups are treated less favourably than others. As such, the concept of exclusion is helpful in promoting an understanding of the experience of people from minority backgrounds or for those who have received inequitable treatment.

The first part of the chapter outlines the theoretical and conceptual frameworks, and starts with a consideration of diversity and equality, placing them within the context of health and social care practice. Next, a summary of approaches to analysing social exclusion is explored in order to highlight how process through the interaction of structures and agency operates. The concept of intersectionality is then introduced to explain how there can be overlapping and multiple forms and experiences of exclusion. This section ends by considering how to put to work the knowledge gained from a consideration of these conceptual frameworks by applying them through and within anti-oppressive practice. The second part of the chapter provides a synopsis of the policy framework, explaining the historical significance of human rights and how the legislative framework developed and operates.

Theoretical and conceptual frameworks

Diversity and equality

The term 'diversity' can refer to many things, including everyday differences such as eye colour, height or style of clothing. The kind of diversity that matters to the professions of health and social care is 'diversity with social significance, diversity that makes real differences to people's lives' (Gaine and Gaylard, 2010: 2). Indeed, the term diversity is increasingly employed to emphasise the differences across and between different groups, but it also points to the require-ment to value such difference rather than see it as a problem to be solved (Thompson, 2012). Throughout these discussions, diversity is based on categories, or social locations, such as gender, sexuality, ethnicity, age, religion, (dis)ability and so on. However, within the UK, in the context of policy and law, the range of available categories is limited and given a legal boundary through the Equality Act (EA) 2010 (see below). The EA defines nine 'protected characteristics' – or specific categories – which are race; disability; sex; gender reassignment; pregnancy and maternity; religion; age; sexuality; and marriage and civil partnership.

Reflection

There are other forms of difference and diversity; for instance, in the wide variety of family configuration (the nuclear family, the reconstituted [or step] family or same-sex house-holds to name a few). There is also a great deal of diversity within the discrete categories offered by the EA. Consider, for example, the diversity of sexuality (in terms of hetero-sexuality, homosexuality, bisexuality and asexuality) or the myriad types of health condi-tions, physical disability and intellectual disability that constitute 'disability'.

Thompson (2012) argues that diversity and difference are the roots of discrimi-nation and as a result various professional bodies have adopted professional codes to promote the values of equality and fairness. For example, in order to practise in the UK, social workers and allied health professionals (such as occu-pational therapists, physical therapists and radiographers) must register with the Health Care and Professionals Council (HCPC). Trainees as well as registered practitioners are required to comply with the *Standards of Conduct, Performance and Ethics* which states:

> You must treat service users and carers as individuals, respecting their privacy and dignity ... You must not discriminate against service users, carers or colleagues by allowing your personal views to affect your professional relationships or the care, treatment or other services that you provide ... You must challenge colleagues if you think that they have discriminated against, or are discriminating against, service users, carers and colleagues. (HCPC, 2016: 5)

Evidently, the view of the law and that of the health and social care professions is that people's backgrounds and individual characteristics should be accepted and discrimination should be challenged and combated. There is a moral and value-based underpinning to this view which also implies the promotion of equality of opportunity and access to services.

Reflection

As noted above in the introduction, the UK is a more 'tolerant' society which 'accepts' diverse people and communities. Diversity also has a positive value as difference enriches our lives, introduces us to new ideas and experiences, and we are encouraged to celebrate difference. Critically reflect on the meaning of the words **'tolerate'** and **'accept'**; would you wish for someone to 'tolerate' or 'accept' you and your difference? Consider how both terms imply a degree of power within the relationship between the person of difference and the person who is accepting or tolerating them. How does this reproduce power hierarchies and inequalities?

Exclusion/Inclusion

The term 'social exclusion' became widely used in policy circles and was placed on the political agenda during New Labour's first term in office. Monro (2005: 43) describes *social exclusion* as 'the way in which certain groups lack the resources to participate in wider society and face barriers to participation', and it infers an included majority and excluded minority. Social exclusion has several dimensions including the *economic* (pertaining to income and employment or resources such as housing or public services); the *social* (for instance, in terms of social participation or the capacity to participate in decision-making processes); or the *political* (citizenship or political rights); and a *spatial* dimension (relating to exclusion at neighbourhood level). These dimensions are not distinct; there are many overlaps and synergies. On the contrary, *social inclusion* may mean that an individual has access to the positive aspects of these dimensions; they enjoy a good level of income and employment, for example. However, a person who is not socially excluded does not necessarily feel included: a person may have income and employment, but may be excluded in terms of the social and spatial (they may be an immigrant who lives in a predominantly white community). On the other hand, they may be 'tolerated' and 'accepted', in other words 'included' to some extent, but this does not imply social connectedness (Taket, 2009).

Clearly the debates are complex and social exclusion is a contested term (Burchardt et al., 2002) as it can refer to exclusion from the labour market, poverty or to more individualised problems which prevent a person from participating in and contributing to society (problems are wide-ranging and may result from, for example, substance misuse, domestic violence, criminal or anti-social behaviour). Thus, it refers to processes and outcomes, rather than being merely a description of the way in which people can become distanced or disconnected from communities and society overall. Ruth Levitas (2005) identified three discourses that are often used to explain social exclusion. The 'Redistributionist Discourse' (RED) highlights that a lack of financial resources creates exclusion from participation in wider society, the implication being that a redistribution of income would address the problem. The 'Social Integrationist Discourse' (SID) focuses on employment as the route to inclusion, suggesting that financial resources alone do not secure inclusion. The 'Moral Underclass Discourse' (MUD) focuses less on structural factors, and emphasises the 'characteristics' and behaviours of the excluded as being the causes of exclusion. While each discourse cannot explain the exclusion/inclusion experienced by all individuals and/or communities, the model offered by Levitas benefits an analysis of different forms of marginalisation as experienced by particular groups in different contexts. Although a simplification, RED and SID focus on the structural barriers to exclusion and suggest that social processes and institutions need to be recalibrated to ensure the inclusion of marginalised groups in society. MUD, on the other hand, is more concerned with the behavioural characteristics of individuals (and groups), holding them responsible for their exclusion.

Intersectionality

Intersectionality is a concept which has been used to understand how people's different social positions overlap (see Crenshaw, 1989). Intersectionality can also be understood as the connections between social divisions (Anthias, 2008) or how different social categories are related to one another (Valentine, 2007). Previously used by critical race theorists and Black Feminists, this concept was developed to understand the multiple and overlapping social positions of Black women with regard to how oppression can be multi-layered and reinforced (Staunæs, 2010). Intersectionality is useful when attempting to understand how multiple social positions can be experienced; however, some have criticised its rigidity and the rather mechanistic way that overlapping social positions are understood to operate (Anthias, 2008; Ahmed, 2015a). Positionality has been presented as a less fixed way of understanding how people's multiple social positions (or locations) are experienced since it takes account of the processes involved in identity construction and ascription (Anthias, 2002; 2008; Ahmed, 2015a). Importantly too, people may be assigned different social positions depending on the context they are in, and also based on their own perceptions of 'who' they are, and when, where and how (Ahmed, 2015a). Intersectionality is conceptually useful when considering marginalisation as it captures multiple and diverse positions: people can occupy more than one social location; for example, they could be young, black and experience mental health problems.

Reflection

Intersectionality refers to the overlapping and multiple 'social locations' that people can inhabit. How does this challenge the portrayal of 'protected characteristics' contained within the Equality Act 2010 as being discrete categories?

The practice framework

Anti-oppressive practice

So far this chapter has explored some key terms and concepts in order to introduce the reader to the ways in which difference, diversity and marginalisation can be understood. More importantly, within the health and social care sector, the way in which this knowledge can be *applied* in real life settings is through a model of anti-oppressive practice (AOP). While the language of AOP has become ubiquitous in social care and social work in particular (Cocker and Hafford-Letchfield, 2014), a precise definition of AOP is contested by the very language adopted in the literature concerned with health and social care. For example, Thompson (2012) employs the umbrella term 'anti-discriminatory practice' (ADP) to include action which is anti-oppressive. Others differentiate ADP and AOP as related, but distinct, concepts. Clifford and Burke (2009) illustrate this in their view of ADP as action which addresses micro, or individual, discrimination whereas AOP is concerned with macro, or wider, systemic problems. In this framework, AOP centres on people whose lives are affected by structural inequalities like poverty, racism, sexism and disablism (Dominelli, 2009). Whichever term is preferred, there are clear overlaps in terms of the need to address inequality and discrimination at both micro and macros levels.

Thompson (2006) offers a conceptual framework for understanding these micro and macro level inequalities which he terms the 'Personal, Social and Cultural' (PCS) model of oppression. While this has been constructed for use in the social work field, there is clearly a value for all practice within the broader remit of 'people work'. Thompson delineates the 'P', 'C' and 'S' thus:

- Personal, or psychological – referring to individual thoughts, feelings and actions that people have (this can include personal prejudices in the form of inflexible attitudes and biases). The 'P' also represents practice (in terms of service provision);

- Community or cultural beliefs – this includes shared ways of viewing the world, and shared actions. Culture also refers to the ways in which communities have shared understandings (consensus), habits and customs and, as such, community has influence over what is set out as 'normative' (commonality);

● Social and structural – this refers to the dynamic network of structural rela-tions and power. The 'S' provides a prompt for considering the institutional-ised and systemic nature of inequality and discrimination along with the social, cultural and political dimension of privilege and influence. (Thomp-son, 2012)

Thompson's analysis underlines the ways in which personal, cultural and social aspects of everyday life interrelate to reproduce and reinforce discrimination and oppression. Adopting the AOP model is one way in which practitioners can be alert to and remain mindful of the way in which power is embedded within and across these systems (including those pertaining to health and social care contexts). However, there is a call to reframe and rethink AOP and ADP frame-works (Rogers, 2013; Cocker and Hafford-Letchfield, 2014) while remaining anchored to the underpinning values of social justice and equality. Rogers (2013) notes how the AOP paradigm tends to be located within normative discourses and thus excludes people and communities who do not conform to dominant versions of ethnicity, gender or sexuality, for example. Mallon (2009) argues that this is easily remedied by extending the knowledge base on margin-alised communities to include practice wisdom derived from professional narra-tives, personal experiences, historical and current political awareness, knowledge of the professional literature, the evidence-base, and theoretical and conceptual analyses. Moreover, rethinking the AOP paradigm would help to respond to the increasing complexity and changing contexts in which we live and remain receptive to the heterogeneity of need displayed by existing communities and those communities impacted by the relatively hidden forms of marginalisation which are exposed in this book. We use the term 'marginalisation' to denote the dynamics and processes which make experiences of accessing health and social care services problematic for less heard groups in society, but it has wider appli-cation. Marginalisation also relates to social status, and can arise through being born into particular groupings in society (for example, ethnic group), but for others it can be acquired through becoming disabled or by changes in the economic system.

Indeed, as service users represent a diverse population, service provision is not always accessible and eligibility is not equal for all people. The chapters in this book provide persuasive accounts of the barriers to accessing services for people who are already marginalised due to their perceived difference, or who have trouble accessing services which do not take into account their particular disability or individual circumstances (see, for example, the case study material in Chapter 4). Furthermore, the practitioners who are employed within the health and social care sector also occupy diverse social locations, but this is not always reflected in the cultures and practices in health and social care. This was the key conclusion of Somerville (2015) who surveyed over 3000 health and social care workers in relation to their attitudes towards lesbian, gay, bisexual and trans people (LGBT), finding homophobic, biphobic and transphobic attitudes to be common and manifest among people working in the sector. Therefore, the drive for AOP continues and the need to draw attention to the needs of marginalised communities underpins the motivation to draw attention to the case studies and communities discussed in this book.

The policy framework

Promoting human rights

Human rights have been present in moral, political and legal analyses and theory for many centuries. However, there is no global consensus about what human rights actually are (Clucas, 2012). For the purpose of this chapter, human rights can be understood as a fundamental characteristic of being human. In the UK, human rights are defined in law through the Human Rights Act 1998 as well as the Equality Act 2010 (the latter is explored more fully below). Both of these are governed and regulated by a state appointed body, the Equality and Human Rights Commission, established in 2007. These Acts can also be mapped against a broader European legal framework which incorporates a commitment to human rights and equality through the institutions of the European Court of Human Rights (ECtHR), the European Court of Justice (ECJ) and the European Union (EU) as well as through treaties and agreements such as the European Convention on Human Rights (ECHR). The relevant human rights that have influenced equality legislation are as follows:

- Article 8.1. Everyone has the right to respect for his private and family life, his home and his correspondence.

- Article 9.1. Everyone has the right to freedom of thought, conscience and religion; this right includes freedom to change his (sic) religion or belief and freedom, either alone or in community with others and in public or private, to manifest his (sic) religion or belief, in worship, teaching, practice and observance.

- Article 14. Prohibition of discrimination on the enjoyment of the Convention rights and freedoms. (ECHR/CoE, undated)

The UK government incorporated the ECHR through the implementation of the Human Rights Act (HRA) 1998. Effective since 2000, the HRA requires all legislation to be compatible with the ECHR. The role of the ECtHR is to hear cases and appeals brought forward using the human rights and equality legislation. Thus the ECtHR has an important role to play in terms of making human rights decisions which can act as catalyst for further changes in domestic (UK) law. Examples of this include the ECtHR ruling in January 2013 against two British Christians who claimed that they were fired because they would not work with gay couples. A marriage registrar for London's Islington Borough Council, and a relationship counsellor, who refused to give sex advice to gay couples, lost their anti-discrimination case. At the same time, in a religious discrimination case the ECtHR ruled in favour of an employee of British Airways who had brought the case claiming that her employer had forced her to stop wearing a cross around her neck. ECHR judges agreed by five votes to two that the employee had experienced religious discrimination.

However, some authors argue that any legislative shift at EU member state level is constrained by the dominant ideological machinery of that country as Woodiwiss observes that:

> Each society will tend to produce a human rights regime that suits itself, especially in the sense that it interferes as little as possible with the prevailing disposition of power. Thus, although human rights regimes provide protections for the weaker parties in sets of social relations, there are always modes of protection available that are less disruptive of the status quo than others, and these less disruptive regimes are those that tend to become established. (Woodiwiss, 2005: 5)

Inasmuch, within individual countries human rights and equality legislation can serve to perpetuate discrimination and exclusion as institutional arrangements and the application of laws 'may conceal and even perpetuate social inequalities' (Waites, 2003: 641). Therefore, an analysis of human rights and equality in the UK must take into account the relationships of power at micro and structural levels.

The legislative framework

Challenging discrimination: the Equality Act 2010

The Equality Act (EA) 2010 came into force from October 2010. It replaced an amalgam of legislation and policy including the Sex Discrimination Act 1975, the Race Relations Act 1976 and the Disability Discrimination Act 1995 as well as their subsequent revisions. In fact, in total there are nine pieces of primary legislation and over 100 pieces of secondary legislation that were incorporated into the new Act. Thus, the EA is a harmonisation of existing law to provide a modernised, single legal framework. It is the most significant piece of equality legislation in many years (EHRC, 2015). The EA simplifies, streamlines and strengthens the law. It also gives individuals greater protection from unfair discrimination through the addition of new categories for protection (such as religion and age), making it more holistic and reaching further than previous equality law.

The categories of discrimination have been extended and, in essence, the EA delineates the different ways in which it is unlawful to treat somebody offering legal redress to people under the nine categories of 'protected characteristics' (age, disability, gender reassignment, marriage and civil partnership, pregnancy and maternity, race, religion or belief, sex and sexual orientation). The Equality Act 2010 also extended the various types of discrimination that can be drawn upon for legal redress. These are:

- *Direct discrimination* – where someone is treated less favourably than another person because of a protected characteristic. For instance, discrimination would have occurred if a gay married couple were refused a stay in a hotel because of their sexual orientation;

- *Associative discrimination* – this is direct discrimination perpetrated against someone because they are associated with another person who possesses a protected characteristic. For example, the parent of a disabled child;

- *Discrimination based on perception* – this is direct discrimination against someone because others think that s/he possess a particular protected characteristic. They do not necessarily have to possess the characteristic, just be perceived to. For example, discrimination can take place if a health and social care worker does not allow a person to make their own decisions about their care based on a belief about age and capacity, but without evidence to corroborate their actions;

- *Indirect discrimination* – this can occur when there is a rule or policy that applies to everyone but disadvantages a person with a particular protected characteristic. For instance, in the case of a rule at a local golf club where only men can attend a golf club bar, this is gender-based discrimination;

- *Harassment* – this is behaviour that is deemed as offensive by the recipient. Employees are able to make a complaint about the behaviour that they find offensive even if it is not directed at them (for example, a woman who works in an all-male environment can experience harassment if there is pornography in the workplace);

- *Victimisation* – this occurs when someone is treated badly because they have made or supported a grievance made under this legislation. For example, if someone has made a claim under the Act previously, but is then refused a promotion because of their previous actions. (EHRC, 2016)

Criticisms can be found, however; for example, see Chapter 6 in this book which highlights the normative ideology used to underpin the way the EA addresses gender reassignment. More specifically, in this case the EA can be critiqued for the way in which it defines gender identity in conservative terms as being constituted by the two fixed categories of male and female (Chapter 6 shows how gender is not necessarily limited to these categories for some people). More broadly, while the EA seeks to determine equality norms, it is also limited in its attempts to respect the human rights of the whole population by its approach to defining equality through the use of a taxonomy of 'protected characteristics' (Clucas, 2012). This limited taxonomy runs counter to the argument for universalism in terms of human rights. Furthermore, Clucas (2012) claims that:

> While formally equal human rights are not the last word for those seeking to obtain social and institutional equality, formal legal inequality at least permits, and arguably encourages, discriminatory practice. (Clucas, 2012: 939)

Clucas argues that there is no formal equality in the EA, using an example of the limitations of equal rights resulting from the interrelationship of some of the protected characteristic categories. Clucas uses a case study – the hypothetical situation of a gay man, who is in a same-sex civil partnership and the criteria to become a bishop within the Church of England – to demonstrate how, while religion, sexual orientation and marriage/civil partnership are protected characteristics, the policy that gay men who are sexually active cannot be proposed as a candidate for promotion to the post of bishop illustrates a tension in the distinction of and relationship between protected characteristics. This tension, or bias, Clucas (2012: 940) argues 'illuminates the social values and understandings that underlie this legislative accommodation of competing human rights'.

Despite this critique, the EA incorporates another important provision, as under section 149 of the Act, the Public Sector Equality Duty (the Equality Duty) was created. The Equality Duty seeks to harmonise the previous gender, race and disability equality duties and extends protection to the new protected characteristics contained within the EA. The Equality Duty makes it easier for employers and companies to understand their responsibilities. It also sets a new standard for those who provide public services to treat everyone with dignity and respect. Those subject to the Equality Duty (including public sector) are required to comply with the three aims of the duty and must have due regard to:

i. eliminating unlawful discrimination, harassment and victimisation as well as other conduct prohibited by the EA;

ii. advancing equality of opportunity between people who share a protected characteristic and those who do not;

iii. fostering good relations between those who share a protected characteristic and those who do not. (EHRC, 2015b)

Case study: **Joe**

For the past 18 months, Joe has lived in Oak Lodge, a supported housing scheme for people with learning disabilities. Joe is 20 years old. He has a learning disability and a sight impairment which means that he has limited vision in one eye. Joe attended a local school and college for young people with additional needs and has some friends that he keeps in touch with. During his adolescence, Joe spent most of his time with his best friend, Billy, who lives next door to Joe's family. Billy is eighteen years old. He is openly gay and frequents the local gay village in a nearby city. He has taken Joe on a number of occasions; experiences which Joe thoroughly enjoyed (he loves music and dancing). In two months' time Joe will be 21 years old. He wants to have a 21st birthday party at a bar in the gay village but Joe's parents are not happy and they have booked the local church hall for a big party with family and friends.

Joe's parents have spoken to his support worker, Jim, who is trying to persuade Joe to go along with his parent's plan. In addition, when Billy has taken Joe out to the gay village, the pair have always returned later than arranged with Oak Lodge. Some of the support staff are not keen on Billy and feel that he is a bad influence (although none of them really know him). On one occasion, Joe's support worker, Jim, had a minor argument with Joe over his desire to have a tattoo. Jim also does not like Billy and admitted to other support staff at Oak Lodge that he did not feel that it was appropriate for Joe to go to gay bars. One of the staff members, Sue (a gay woman), took offence at this. She felt that Jim, and others in the team, were making judgements about Joe's involvement with gay people and the scene, rather than prioritising Joe's self-confidence and development as a young adult. She also felt that support staff should encourage Joe to develop independent living skills and maintain relationships which he identified as important. Sue reported the incident to the organisation's human resources department.

- Do you believe that Joe has experienced discrimination?

- If so, identify (1) how you think Joe has experienced discrimination, (2) any relevant protected characteristics and (3) the types of discrimination he may have encountered.

- Also, do you think Jim's employer has a 'public duty' to take action and if so, in what ways?

The case study indicates that Joe may have experienced *associative discrimination*. This is direct discrimination perpetrated against someone because they are associated with another person (Billy) who possesses a protected characteristic (sexual orientation) and/or even *discrimination based on perception* – direct discrimination against someone (Joe) because others (Jim) think that s/he possess a particular protected characteristic (sexual orientation). In addition, as Oak Lodge operates under the remit of the local authority, it is considered to be a public body which is subject to the public sector Equality Duty. This means that the human resources department should consider Sue's claims within the context of the three aims of the duty as detailed above.

Conclusion

This chapter has introduced the conceptual, theoretical, legal and policy frameworks which shape discussions of diversity and exclusion. In so doing, we have established the context in which the discussions in the following chapters are placed. In the following chapter Morton and Myers develop this discussion further by highlighting how health and social care organisations have attempted to address diversity through inclusive practice, and how there can be unintended consequences of highlighting difference.

Recommended reading

- Crenshaw, K. (1989) *Demarginalizing the Intersection of Race and Sex: A Black Feminist Critique of Antidiscrimination Doctrine, Feminist Theory, and Antiracist Politics*, University of Chicago Legal Forum.

- EHRC (2015a) *Equality Act Guidance, Codes of Practice and Technical Guidance.* Available at: www.equalityhumanrights.com/en/advice-and-guidance/equality-act-guidance.

- EHRC (2015b) *The Public Sector Equality Duty.* Available at: www.equalityhumanrights.com/about-us/about-commission/equality-and-diversity/public-sector-equality-duty.

- Levitas, R. (2nd Edition) (2005) *The Inclusive Society? Social Exclusion and New Labour*, UK, Palgrave Macmillan.

Relevant web links

- **www.equalityhumanrights.com** The Equality and Human Rights Commission states 'we live in a country with a long history of upholding people's rights, valuing diversity and challenging intolerance. The EHRC seeks to maintain and strengthen this heritage while identifying and tackling areas where there is still unfair discrimination or where human rights are not being respected.

- **www.fawcettsociety.org.uk** The Fawcett Society is an organisation in the United Kingdom that campaigns for women's rights.

- **www.coe.int/en** The Council of Europe is a regional intergovernmental organisation whose goal is to promote human rights and democracy. The most well-known body of the Council of Europe is the European Court of Human Rights which enforces the European Convention on Human Rights.

- **http://fra.europa.eu/en** The European Union Fundamental Rights Agency was established with a vision to help make fundamental rights a reality for everyone in the European Union.

References

Ahmed, A. (2015a) *Retiring to Spain: Women's Narratives of Nostalgia, Belonging and Community.* Bristol: Policy Press.

_____(2015b) UK migration and elderly care regimes. In U,. Karl and S. Torres (eds) *Ageing in Contexts of Migration.* London: Sage.

Anthias, F. (2002) Where do I belong?: Narrating identity and translocational positionality, *Ethnicities,* 2(4): 491–515.

_____(2008) Thinking through the lens of translocational positionality: an intersectionality frame for understanding identity and belonging, *Translocations: Migration and Social Change,* 4(1): 5–20.

Burchardt, T., Le Grand, J. and Piachaud, D. (2002) Introduction. In J. Hills, J. Le Grand and D. Piachard (eds) *Understanding Social Exclusion.* Oxford: Oxford University Press.

Cocker, C. and Hafford-Letchfield, T. (eds) (2014) *Rethinking Anti-Discriminatory & Anti-Oppressive Theories for Social Work Practice.* Basingstoke: Palgrave Macmillan.

Clifford, D. and Burke, B. (2009) *Anti-Oppressive Ethics and Values in Social Work.* Basingstoke: Palgrave Macmillan.

Crenshaw, K. (1989) *Demarginalizing the Intersection of Race and Sex: A Black Feminist Critique of Antidiscrimination Doctrine, Feminist Theory, and Antiracist Politics.* University of Chicago Legal Forum.

Clucas, R. (2012) Religion, sexual orientation and the Equality Act 2010: Gay Bishops in the Church of England negotiating rights against discrimination. *Sociology,* 46(5): 936–950.

Department of Work and Pensions (DWP) (2014) Disability Facts and Figures. Available at: www.gov.uk/government/statistics/disability-facts-and-figures (accessed 11 February 2016).

Dominelli, L. (2009) Anti-oppressive practice: The challenges of the twenty-first century. In R. Adams, L. Dominelli and M. Payne (eds) *Social Work: Themes, Issues and Debates* (3rd edn). Basingstoke: Palgrave Macmillan, pp.49–64.

ECHR/CoE (undated) European Convention of Human Rights. Strasbourg: ECHR/CoE.

EHRC (2015a) *Equality Act Guidance, Codes of Practice and Technical Guidance.* Available at: www.equalityhumanrights.com/legal-and-policy/legislation/equality-act-2010/equality-act-guidance-codes-practice-and-technical-guidance (accessed 11 February 2016).

EHRC (2015b) *The Public Sector Equality Duty.* Available at: www.equalityhumanrights.com/about-us/about-commission/equality-and-diversity/public-sector-equality-duty (accessed 11 February 2016).

EHRC (2016) *Your rights under Equality Act 2010*. Available at: www.equalityhuman rights.com/en/advice-and-guidance/your-rights-under-equality-act-2010#h1 (accessed 26 June 2016).

Gaine, C. and Gaylard, D. (2010) Equality, difference and diversity. In C. Gaine (ed.) *Equality and Diversity in Social Work Practice*. London: Learning Matters.

HCPC (2016) Standards of conduct, performance and ethics. Available at: www.hcpc-uk. org/assets/documents/10004EDFStandardsofconduct,performanceandethics.pdf (accessed 15 February 2016).

Levitas, R. (2005) *The Inclusive Society? Social Exclusion and New Labour* (2nd edn). Basing-stoke: Palgrave Macmillan.

Mallon, G.P. (2009) Knowledge for practice with transgender and gender variant youth. In G.P. Mallon (ed.) *Social Work Practice with Transgender and Gender Variant Youth* (2nd edn). London: Routledge.

Monro, S. (2005) *Gender Politics: Citizenship, Activism and Sexual Diversity*. London: Pluto Press.

ONS (2015) *Annual Survey of Hours and Earnings, 2015 Provisional Results*, Table 16. Available at: www.ons.gov.uk/ons/publications/re-reference-tables.html?edition=tcm%3A77-400803 (accessed 11 February 2016).

Rogers, M. (2013) *TransForming Practice: Understanding Trans People's Experience of Domestic Abuse and Social Care Agencies*. PhD thesis, University of Sheffield, UK.

Somerville, C. (2015) *Unhealthy attitudes: the treatment of LGBT people within health and social care services*. London: Stonewall.

Staunæs (2010) Where have all the subjects gone? Bringing together the concepts of intersectionality and subjectification, *NORA – Nordic Journal of Feminist and Gender Research*,11(2): 101–110.

Taket, A.R. (2009) *Theorising Social Exclusion*. London: Routledge.

Thompson, N. (2006) *Anti-discriminatory Practice* (4th edn). Basingstoke: Palgrave Macmillan.

_____(2012) *Anti-Discriminatory Practice: Equality, Diversity and Social Justice* (5th edn). Basingstoke: Palgrave Macmillan.

Waites, M. (2003) Equality at last? Homosexuality, heterosexuality and the age of consent in the United Kingdom. *Sociology*, 37(4): 637–655.

Woodiwiss, A. (2005) *Human Rights*. London: Routledge.

2

IDENTITY, DIFFERENCE AND THE MEANING OF 'CULTURE' IN HEALTH AND SOCIAL CARE PRACTICE

Julie Morton and Steve Myers

Chapter overview: **key messages**

- Health and social care services have become increasingly aware of diversity and the need for inclusive practice.
- This has taken particular forms that have consequences for service users.
  Respect for identity and difference has been seen as integral to anti-discriminatory practice and cultural competence approaches.
- Despite benign intentions, practices can reinforce exclusion through the production of new understandings of 'difference' and/or 'need'.
- Reflexive practice approaches may be more helpful in understanding individuals in context and consequently provide more effective interventions.

Introduction

Public services generally within the UK have become increasingly aware that the population they serve is not homogenous. This is due to both demographic changes through migration and an increasing recognition that there are social category differences which impact on how people experience service delivery. Health and social care services in particular have made efforts to provide services that are responsive to the often different needs of groups that have found themselves marginalised and excluded by mainstream service construction and delivery. The Equality Act 2010 has led to further development of policies and processes to promote inclusion, for example through the creation of an Equality and Diversity Council for the NHS in England (NHS, undated) and the introduction of guiding principles for social care (Skills for Care, 2013). Social Work (our professional background) has developed anti-discriminatory practice and incorporated the notion of cultural competence in its core values, reflecting the commitment to address social injustice. This is usually articulated through the terminology of diversity and difference.

The intentions motivating these initiatives are laudable and benign, recognising that serious injustice and harm has been done to those who have been marginalised and stigmatised through actions and inactions. The approach has been to redress this injustice through policies and practices that view difference not as problematic but worthy of recognition and to be valued. However, we argue that this understanding of difference produces new forms of exclusionary processes based on essentialised ideas of the person located within the category. The case studies provided in this chapter show how practice often 'essentialises' people and that there are consequences of this. For example, essentialised ideas about gender assume that there are sets of characteristics about men and women that are 'natural'. Women may be viewed as caring and nurturing (which they can of course be) but rather than seeing these simply as essential, pre-existing characteristics of being female, they may be influenced by social expectations of what it is to be a woman in society. Fixed notions of identity and culture assume there are group characteristics that can be found, understood and judged, which is a process of *othering* that presumes, creates and accentuates differences; a new form of discrimination. In health and social care this is often couched in terms of needs, where socially constructed groups are thought of in terms of their differences from the norm.

We choose to use the term *culture* to describe the ways in which difference is thought of, partly because there are discussions about meeting the cultural needs of socially constructed groups through *cultural competence*, and partly because this term lends itself to existing post-colonial theorising about how culture is exoticised and eroticised. The chapter develops some of the negative and/or problematic consequences of dominant understandings of difference and identity. We use ethnicity and sexuality to provide examples of how these processes work in everyday health and social care practices.

Concepts of difference, identity and 'culture'

Services are often delivered in ways that place individuals into categories. For example, services for children or older people provide an obvious and typical division in delivery. This can be problematic because in order to meet the criteria for a service, the individual and her/his difficulties must be constructed in a particular way. It is essential that someone can 'tick the right boxes' in order to fulfil the criteria and receive a service. This process also happens with identity. People are placed in categories according to their perceived identity: their 'race', their gender, their sexuality or their class. These then become static ways of defining and working with difference. In this chapter, we want to trouble these categories of difference. We are using ethnicity, 'race' and sexuality to talk about how difference and culture are constructed in everyday practices and some of the consequences of these practices. So we are referring to how health and social care *works* with difference.

Seeing people as belonging to categories in relation to difference has consequences for practice. People are often grouped together in relation to their perceived identity. Identity in turn has been increasingly linked to the idea of 'culture'.

The term 'culture' is difficult to define but usually refers to a whole range of actions, beliefs, communications and values belonging to a social group. However, culture is almost always used in practice to refer to culture that is other than the dominant culture, leading to practice that presumes that, for example, understanding Asian culture is needed in order to work with Asian people or an appreciation of gay culture is necessary in order to fully engage with someone who is lesbian or gay (Yee and Dumbrill, 2003). However, these understandings are often limited and competence in working with these different cultures assumes there is a fixed culture to know about. For example, the complexities and range of Asian cultures are subsumed into a general catch-all category 'Asian' which presumes that there are shared characteristics across very different societies (Park, 2005). What do Indian, Pakistani, Chinese, Indonesian, Muslim, Hindu or Buddhist cultures, all of which are 'Asian', have in common? It would be difficult to imagine truly knowing all the detail of these varied cultural practices so understanding tends to be limited to token aspects, what has been disparagingly called the 'saris, samosas and steel band syndrome' (Sundar and Ly, 2013: 134). As Sakamoto (2007) outlines, this approach also assumes that culture is something that is neutral and apolitical. In this way of thinking, working with other cultures does not require a critical perspective on power and oppression, only knowledge of (superficial) aspects of the culture being viewed. Indeed, Pon (2009) argues that such fixed notions of culture are actually very similar to fixed biological notions of difference, from which most health and social care workers would recoil in horror, yet the move from the exclusionary discourses of biological 'race' (or sexuality) to those of 'culture' is a similar process of constructing difference from an unspoken norm. The focus is still on the object of interest, seeking to understand/control it, avoiding the need to consider how health and social care work(ers) create and reproduce racism, (hetero)sexism and other forms of hegemonic (dominant) power.

Barker (1981) described this shift from biological difference marked by overt racist terminology to cultural difference masked by non-racialised language as *new racism*; the outcome is still an accentuation of difference and being judged against a dominant and unproblematised white culture. This new racism takes for granted the essentialised nature of culture, replacing biological difference with cultural difference and re-creating 'others'. So, in the social world, cultural difference can be used to explain (away) why non-white people may not access services ('Chinese culture means they look after their own older people'), not participate ('Football is not a part of Asian culture') or have familial problems ('Muslim society is very patriarchal'). Whiteness is left unproblematised and unspoken.

We would argue here that this same process is in place (not an exact replication, but with enough similarities to warrant consideration) with sexuality, specifically the ways in which health and social care work thinks about Lesbian, Gay, Bisexual and Transgender (LGBT) people as having separate and different needs. Gay people can be viewed as not yet being introduced to *gay culture* (although we have difficulty in understanding and/or agreeing what this may be), and therefore in denial about their 'true' selves. Heterosexism (the dominance of heterosexuality over other forms of sexuality) is ignored, as the answer is to psychologically and emotionally embrace and develop a personal gay identity, rather than raise questions about oppressive practices that privilege heterosexuality over other sexualities (heteronormativity). This *new homophobia* celebrates a gay identity yet practises exclusion from the mainstream, locating problems in adjustment, access and acceptance of the different culture/identity. Consider the following suggested action for a social worker experiencing homophobia:

> In this situation, it is crucial that Tony has a support group amongst whom he can discuss his predicament, if he is to empower himself... the support group would have to engage with the issues as Tony has experienced them, a process that would be facilitated if its members share identity attributes with him... if he is going to explore issues of homophobia within the group it should contain practising homosexual men and women. (Dominelli, 2002: 103)

The issue we wish to highlight here is that of the prescribed remedy for Tony's problems. The cause of the problem remains unquestioned, and the focus is on supporting Tony to become stronger (empowered) through shared identity attributes. The assumption here is that such identities automatically privilege and propel members into providing support, and that the quality of that support is better than those who are not in the group. This essentialises what are values and attitudes in embodied ways – rather than gaining support from people who have thought about the issue, have values that challenge discrimination, possess personal qualities that are engaging and helpful, we are led to understand that it is the use and deployment of their *bodies* (practising) that enables them to offer appropriate support. We find this approach puzzling and flawed as it restricts and reduces supportive human relationships to those who may (or may not, this advice seems to group every non-heterosexual person together regardless of gender) share erotic similarities. This approach both eroticises and essentialises 'gay' identity, as well as leading to practices that mean that only members of a group can provide the 'correct' services for other members.

Reflection

- How do you define your identity?

- How did you decide to use the words to describe yourself?

- We often fall back on binary opposites, for example, black/white, gay/straight, male/female. How did you use these terms?

- These are ways in which we order the social world and think about social relations, but they are also limiting. They might, for example, suggest an essentialised view of gender or make assumptions about gender differences.

- Ask yourself how you reinforce binaries in your everyday conversations.

Culture and cultural competence

Cultural competence has been defined as the ability to 'deliver professional services in a way that is congruent with behaviour and expectations normative for a given community and that are adapted to suit the specific needs of individuals and families from that community' (Green, 1999: 87). In the US the Child Development Institute (2007) defined cultural competency as 'a set of congruent behaviours, attitudes and policies that enables effective work in cross-cultural situations'. As Pon (2009) points out, these definitions are individualised and avoid any broader socio-political analysis. The idea of cultural competence has been given significance in caring professions but is not without criticism. Harrison and Turner (2011) point out that 'culture' as it is used in social work can lead to one-dimensional or essentialist views of culture rather than it being acknowledged as something that is fluid. Further, 'Given the apparent indeterminacy of culture, it could be argued that coupling it with a more concrete term such as competence is somewhat oxymoronic' (Harrison and Turner, 2011: 335). We would agree that cultural competence is far from straightforward. Harrison and Turner highlight the rather nebulous nature of how 'culture' is understood in health and social care but this is not a common perspective. The more dominant idea is that learning about culture (that is, the culture of others) is necessary. Laird (2008: 39) goes so far as to say that social workers will engage in unintended racism and 'preside over racially discriminatory services until such time as *they learn about other cultures*.' (Our emphasis.) In this chapter we untangle some of the assumptions about culture in day-to-day practice and we demonstrate how the seemingly unproblematic orientation in education and practice to 'learn about cultures' frequently compounds the difficulties and barriers the approach endeavours to dismantle. Cultural competency has become a practitioners' shortcut into understanding identity and difference, fixing and limiting people's experiences rather than understanding them as changing, fluid and situated in time and place.

Consequences for practice

In this section we outline in more detail some of the negative consequences of fixed and dominant understandings of difference and identity. We use ethnicity and sexuality to provide examples of how this works in everyday health and social care practices. Key consequences and difficulties include the following:

Homogeneity: that people's experiences are not unique but are seen as being similar due to common identity and culture.

Limiting understanding: the ways in which people's difficulties are viewed as a product of or result of belonging to that particular category or culture. If practice is focussed on being anti-oppressive, people's difficulties might be assessed as solely being a result of the experiences of discrimination, in this case racism or homophobia. Of course we are not suggesting that structural discrimination (that is, discrimination based on unequal social categories) does not exist, or that racism and homophobia are not powerful and destructive forces. Rather, we argue that discrimination is often understood in limited ways. Furthermore, confining understanding to extreme cases of discrimination ignores the more mundane but prevalent and potentially damaging effects of heteronormative health and social care practices and the privilege and entitlement associated with whiteness. So, for example, anti-oppressive practice would typically adopt an anti-racist stance but this risks ignoring the ways in which practitioners themselves are involved in perpetuating limiting ideas about 'race' in everyday practice.

'Culture' obfuscating assessment of difficulties: difficulties are viewed as arising from within the particular culture or as a result of not adjusting to a particular culture. In this process an individual's difficulties can be seen as arising from, for example, 'oppressive' Muslim culture or due to the individual not having accepted their own culture, or having to conform to gay culture or as a result of the individual not being able to adjust to their culture. Assigning people to specific categories of difference tends to frame difficulties in particular ways. It is ironic that in health and social care work where empowerment is at the core of professional values, difference is largely viewed as giving rise to difficulties rather than experienced as positive or life-affirming. Similarly, where autonomy and independence are meant to be promoted, the resilience people demonstrate when they have experienced discrimination is rarely acknowledged.

Constructing minority needs: people are viewed as having needs or difficulties which have arisen purely from belonging to a particular group. These 'minority' needs mean that identities become fixed and reified through practice. In a minority model, needs are defined by practitioners rather than identified by the individual experiencing the difficulties.

Differences in experience or identity should of course be acknowledged but ideas about difference in professional practice need to be scrutinised and problematised. Dupre (2012: 180) writing about cultural competence in relation to disability has suggested that there should be two important assumptions in the politics of difference. First, that the boundaries of groups are viewed as 'relational, fluid, ambiguous and permeable', and second, that this approach to difference would acknowledge that groups (and here we are referring to the ways in which groups or categories are defined by sexuality or race) develop their own identities rather than being classified by definitions and practices which are imposed by the dominant culture.

Alternative ways of viewing difference for practitioners

Instead of viewing categories such as race and sexuality as static, we think it is much more helpful to analyse how health and social care practitioners and practices are active in constructing identities for individuals. Professional discourses such as cultural competency or anti-oppressive practice are usually left unexamined. However, these professional discourses lead to perspectives which may not take into account what assumptions are being made, what is being left out of understandings, what practitioners consider to be important and why. In other words, the objectives of cultural competence and anti-oppressive practice may actually close down the potential for reflexive practice.

There is a key difficulty with the concept of cultural competence specifically and the traditional ways of understanding difference in health and social care practice more generally. This is that the requirement to become competent in the culture of 'others' does not imply a corresponding consideration of the practitioner's understanding of difference. Though there may be a rather individualised approach advocated in literature in which practitioners are viewed as needing to reflect on their own values and assumptions, there is less emphasis on how practitioners might ask reflexive questions of their own conceptualisations of difference. In Fook's model of analysing practice, an essential part of the critically reflective process is the unearthing of assumptions (Fook and Gardener, 2013; Fook, 2002). This unearthing of the practitioner's assumptions is potentially more helpful in trying to understand what is important for the individual.

Rather than fixing culture, it would be seen along with identity as contextual, unfixed and fluid. In other words, being different rather depends on the social, political and historical context one finds oneself in (Hall, 1997).

Education in health and social care often requires students to be reflective (soul-baring) with the underlying assumption that reflective accounts are help-ful in that they access hidden concerns and offer a deeper understanding of practice (Taylor, 2003). In our experience, reflective accounts can only do this if they are further analysed, they are not in themselves 'true' or necessarily able to assist improved practice understandings. In relation to thinking about culture and competency in day-to-day health and social care practice, a reflective approach in itself is inadequate.

Anti-discriminatory practice (in social work in particular) has addressed the role of power in practice (Thompson, 2012; Dominelli, 2002). Professional dis-courses assume taken-for-granted ideas of difference and culture. Aspects of identity and difference are *a priori* – they are already there, they exist indepen-dently from observation and from the lived experience of patients and service-users. Such professional discourses can result in identity and difference being operationalised rather than understood in contexts. Fook and Gardener (2007: 35) suggest that the deconstruction of practice required for critical reflection offers the possibility for us to unearth the ways in which we are all involved in constructing power through our participation in dominant discourses.

Our preferred approach to practice in general and to thinking about culture and difference in particular is reflexive rather than reflective. We propose that a reflexive approach is an alternative way of making sense of the contingent, fluid and contextually situated experiences of service users. It is important to first explain what we mean by a reflexive approach. At its simplest, reflexivity refers to self-reflection, a level of self-awareness in what one is doing. Though it is an intellectual activity, for reflexivity to be purposeful it needs to be more than 'intellectual introspection' (Bourdieu and Wacquant, 1992: 40). D'Cruz et al. (2007) carried out a review of the different definitions of reflexivity within the context of social work. Three variations in the conceptualisation of the term were identified. In the first variation, reflexivity means simply individualistic reflection about social problems in the context of complex practice. The second variation focuses on the activity of reflection on a dynamic relationship between feelings and thoughts. In the third variation, reflexivity involves reflections on how knowledge and theory about practice are generated. This third variation seems to resonate with Bourdieu's 'epistemic reflexivity', which described a process of identifying the ways in which one's interpretations are located within a particular discourse or discourses. For health and social care work then, epis-temic reflexivity in practice might lead a worker to question the professional discourses which dominate (and/or limit) practice or our ways of understanding the situations we are presented with. We would suggest that though this is an intellectual activity, it is not simply theoretical in the sense of abstract. In a health and social work context reflexivity offers potential for understanding difference and diversity in ways which can lead to helpful interventions. Bourdieu highlighted a hazard of reflexivity in sociological research when he talked about inquiry into social practices becoming abstracted from their context, losing sight of the problems to be addressed or solved (Bourdieu, 2000). In a similar way, when inquiring or making sense of practice situations, it is important not to lose sight of the context in which difficulties or problems are occurring. For us, a reflexive approach in practice comes with a corresponding obligation for the practitioner to question and challenge traditional or dominant practices in context and to maintain a focus on how to overcome difficulties.

Working with difference in health and social care case studies

We are aware that case studies can be problematic as a learning tool and can appear to caricature both difficulties and individuals' experiences. Use of case studies can imply that there are correct and incorrect ways of responding to cases and this is dependent on getting the 'case-formulation' right. This carries a corresponding assumption, which is that the problem is with the individual. These are short case studies presented without context and designed with specific learning effects in mind. We are offering the case studies as a direct route in to discussion of these complex topics. They are intended to provoke discussion and the discussion following is intended to be the start of a conversations that the reader can continue. To illustrate this we present case studies of how practitioners might commonly respond to situations in practice, we outline some consequences of these responses and then analyse the case studies adopting a reflexive approach.

Case study 1

James is 15 and has stopped attending school. He has become quite withdrawn and spends a lot of time in his bedroom. Following concerns about his mental health, he is seen by a specialist young people's health worker who recognises that James is exhibiting symptoms of depression that may be linked to his confusion about his sexuality. When asked, James says that he thinks he may be gay, although he appears to lack confidence about this. The worker thinks that James is having difficulties adjusting and has not yet come to terms with his true sexual identity, due to the oppressive nature of our society. James is encouraged to join a gay youth group to help him gain support in coming out in a positive way.

James thanks the worker for their suggestion, but decides not to take this up as he sees the issue as being the bullying behaviour towards him by other children at school, rather than his problem. The worker is concerned that James may be in denial about his identity.

Interrogating the practitioner's assessment

The practitioner places James's sexuality as an issue of primary significance in the assessment of his difficulties, supported by various social, psychological and psychiatric knowledges. In her formulation of James's difficulties, his difficulties are derived from a particular construction of sexuality. He is *confused;* he hasn't *adjusted* to being gay or come to terms with his *true sexuality*. These ways of thinking locate the problem as an internalised one within James, premised on notions of harm and deficit that require addressing through affirmation of his identity.

Problematising this assessment

A reflexive practitioner might reflect on how helpful it is to pathologise James's problems. S/he might interrogate the notion of true sexuality and consider this as othering. After all, what would true sexuality look like? How would we know when he had adjusted to it? The social aspects of the case are hardly considered. By this, we do not mean addressing the social aspect in that James could be referred to a youth group. We are referring to the day-to-day social relations in James's world which may impact on him; for example, the everyday heteronormative practices in the school context where he experiences the bullying behaviour of pupils, which may or may not be directly linked to his sexuality.

Consequences

The practitioner's formulation has not addressed James's problems; indeed it could be argued that a consequence would be to compound them. Of course, in this scenario, James is able to challenge the practitioner, which may or may not happen in reality.

Alternative ways of understanding

A reflexive practitioner might have been aware of and questioned the dominant discourses of sexuality which exist in practice and addressed her/himself more to the particular context of James's world. Social and healthcare tends to view gay sexuality as something that needs to be adjusted to, which would not be the case for heterosexuality. The social consequences of and responsibility for homophobia are largely ignored in practice, while social work literature (for example) on lesbian and gay mental distress has failed to document 'the abundant evidence of homophobia's existence other than in the minds of lesbians and gay men and leaves unexplored the logic and practice of heterosexual people's homophobia' (Jeyasingham, 2008: 144).

A reflexive approach here might have led to a more helpful intervention which focused not on James's psychological shortcomings but on working at the social level, at school, from where the bullying behaviour emanated.

Case study 2

Sahida is a lone parent raising three children. She left her husband several years ago following sustained domestic violence from him. Her eldest son has committed a sexual offence, which has led to social work involvement in the family. During the assessment Sahida talks about the struggles she has had with alcohol and gambling, and her rejection of the family and culture she came from. Sahida says that she had very little support from her family and community so decided to make a different life for her and her children. She is deeply worried about her son and wants help with his sexualised behaviour. The social worker is concerned that Sahida may be experiencing trauma and loss from rejecting her family and community, losing her identity and making her less resilient in managing her son's behaviour. Concern is also expressed that her son is following her behaviour in rejecting the Asian community and embracing Western values. It is suggested that Sahida attends counselling to help integrate her feelings of trauma and loss and to help regain a positive sense of ethnic identity. This will then increase her emotional resilience and enable her to support her son.

Sahida rejects this as another attempt to blame her for her son's behaviour and demands practical assistance in managing him. The social worker is worried that she is only dealing with the presenting problems and not able to resolve the underlying causes.

Interrogating the practitioner's assessment

The practitioner here is focusing on the issue of ethnicity/culture as a defining factor in the construction of the problems. Again we see a strong psychological element in understanding the service user, utilising notions of 'trauma and loss' from psychoanalytic theorising to the decisions made by Sahida. There are notions of inherent strength in having a strong *ethnic identity* and concerns that lack of this undermines the potential for self-actualisation and in providing adequate care for her children.

Problematising the assessment

In this scenario ethnicity and culture are seen as key determinants of the person, their situation and any solutions to the problems. The focus of direct practice is through this lens, which may close down other ways of understanding and responding. What is obscured in this analysis are gender relations and self-determination, paradoxically viewing what could be an empowering decision to remove herself from domestic violence as being damaging to her personal and cultural identity. Her implied *cultural deficit* has become the issue, requiring input to restore it to its *correct* level, which will then (somehow) provide resilience against further difficulties. Culture has become an internalised and psychologised problem and the importance of social context is reduced to its impact on her emotional state, leading to practice that tries to rectify individual pathology. The notion of *presenting problems* locates the worker as the diagnostic expert in defining what the *real* problems are, marginalising Sahida's account as being the product of lack of insight, false consciousness or cultural deficit. In this scenario it is hard to see how such an approach would be taken with white indigenous (UK) people as it is premised on a rather idealised notion of *other* culture.

Consequences

Sahida finds the worker's assessment unhelpful as it does not assist her with her immediate difficulties of managing her son's behaviour.

Alternative ways of understanding

Sahida has demonstrated strengths in her actions that appear to have been overlooked. Further discussion about how she managed to remove herself and her children from the domestically violent situation would be useful, recognising the effort this must have taken and celebrating her achievements. The challenge of raising three children on her own is marginalised, and financial, housing and employment issues are absent from the assessment. Hearing what she has to say about her situation, rather than presuming that culture is at the centre of this, allows for a narrative that has more meaning for Sahida.

Reflection

- Consider what your preferred way of understanding people is.
- How does this assist you in explaining their situation?

- How helpful is this and why?
- What are the limitations of this way of thinking?
- What/who do you exclude in your assessments by adopting your particular perspective?
- Which explanations dominate your thinking and formulations?

Key messages for health and social care practice

Using a cultural competence approach in health and social care leads to a number of difficulties. In assessment of needs, the 'deficit' or difficulty can be framed as emanating from the culture itself (whether gay culture or culture in relation to ethnicity) or as the (mis)adaption of the individual to their culture. Homogeneity is assumed where it may not exist. Minority groups are assumed to have discrete, particular needs and there is an assumption that the individual can be understood through a 'group' identity.

Subsequent interventions or helping can miss more mundane and practical difficulties which might need addressing, for example, bullying, poverty, marginalisation or isolation. Alternative perspectives on sexuality may be more helpful in general, for example, viewing sexuality as sets of social relations through which understandings of relationships, sex and sexual difference are negotiated. This would mean that sexuality was not simply an aspect of personal identity or limited to the erotic, private or informal spheres (Morton, Jeyasingham and Hicks, 2013).

Knowledge systems in professional practice discourses such as cultural competence generally relate to identities that are not white. The difficulty with this is that instead of challenging racism and structural inequalities, practices may inadvertently reproduce white centrality, othering the experiences of individuals and communities that are not white. This is what Dyer (1997) argues when talking about the importance of making whiteness visible or seeing it as 'strange'. If our practitioner gaze is always on cultures which are not white then whiteness is invisible. Whiteness then comes to mean the human condition, defining normality. In the othering of non-white cultures, cultural competency approaches in relation to ethnicity can have the opposite effect of the inclusive practice they aim to achieve because they produce an idea of what is 'normal' and what is 'other'. A reflexive approach to identity and difference would focus instead on interactions in everyday practice and examine how these:

- Create, perpetuate and bring about limited ways of viewing sexuality and sexual norms
- Create, perpetuate and bring about limited ways of viewing race

This would involve practitioners thinking about their own perceptions of identity and difference, their own ways of thinking about health and well-being and, importantly, having regard for the ways in which they 'work' in their professional contexts.

Conclusion

We have questioned whether *culture* as an umbrella term is helpful given the ways it is used in practice in health and social care. This is in part because of its use in practice, referring to cultures *other than* the dominant culture ('race' or sexuality). We propose an alternative approach to inclusion and diversity with reflexivity at its core. There are difficulties with assessments of problems when they are seen as being outside political and social spheres. Problems become pathologised. Banks (2013) has articulated the ways in which ethical issues in practice focus on the individual or family and not on critiques of social policy or on the health and social care worker taking political action. We would argue that reflexive practice requires a focus on the dominant social discourses in society and in the health and social care professions. While it may seem obvious that individuals' difficulties do not occur in a social vacuum, dominant ideas about identity in the professions also require critique. Professional case formulations are steeped in everyday assumptions about identity and culture, some of which we have highlighted in this chapter. Practice which fails to problematise these assumptions, a non-reflexive practice, means that individuals' problems can be compounded by services rather than alleviated.

Recommended reading

- Fook, J. (2002) *Social Work: Critical Theory and Practice.* London. Sage. Contains useful chapters on identity and on how we can deconstruct our practice to unearth limiting assumptions and reconstruct more helpful formulations.

- Horvat, L., Horey, D., Romios, P. and Kis-Rigo, J. (2014) *Cultural Competence Education for Health Professionals.* Cochrane Database of Systematic Reviews 2014, Issue 5. This is a recent Cochrane Collaboration review of cultural competence education and its effects in healthcare.

- Taylor, C. and White, S. (2000) *Practising Reflexivity in Health and Social Care: Making Knowledge.* Buckingham. Open University Press.

Relevant web links

- www.youngstonewall.org.uk/
- www.basw.co.uk
- www.scie.org.uk

References

Banks, S. (2013) Ethics. In I. Ferguson, M. Lavalette and S. Banks. (2013). *Ethics: Critical and Radical Debates in Social Work*. Bristol: Policy Press.

Barker, M. (1981) *The New Racism*. London: Junction Books.

Bourdieu, P. (1990) *The Logic of Practice*. Cambridge: Political Press.

_____(2000) *Pascalian Meditations*. Cambridge: Polity Press.

Bourdieu, P. and Waquant, L. (1992) *An Invitation to Reflexive Sociology*. Chicago: University of Chicago Press.

D'Cruz, H., Gillingham, P. and Melendez, S. (2007) Reflexivity, its meaning and relevance for social work: a critical review of the literature. *British Journal of Social Work*, 37: 73–90.

Dominelli, L. (2002) *Anti-Oppressive Social Work Theory and Practice*. Basingstoke: Palgrave Macmillan.

Dupré, M. (2012) Disability culture and cultural competency in social work. *Social Work Education*, 31(2): 168–183.

Dyer, R. (1997) *White*. London: Routledge.

Fook, J. (2002) *Social Work: Critical Theory and Practice*. London: Sage.

Fook, J. and Gardner, F. (2007) *Practising Critical Reflection: A Resource Handbook*. Maidenhead: Open University Press.

_____(2013) *Critical Reflection in Context: Applications in Health and Social Care*. London: Routledge.

Green, J.W. (1999) *Cultural Awareness in the Human Services*. Needham Heights, MA: Alyn & Bacon.

Hall, S. (1997) *Representation: Cultural Representations and Signifying Practices*. London: Sage.

Harrison, G. and Turner, R. (2011) Being a culturally competent social worker: Making sense of a murky concept in practice: *British Journal of Social Work*, 41: 333–350.

NHS (undated) *The NHS Equality and Diversity Hub*. Available at: www.england.nhs.uk/ourwork/gov/equality-hub/edc/ (accessed 12 November 2015).

Jeyasingham, D. (2008) Knowledge/ignorance and the construction of sexuality in social work education. *Social Work Education*, 27: 138–151.

Laird, S.E. (2008) *Anti-Oppressive Social Work: A Guide for Developing Cultural Competence*. London: Sage

Morton, J., Jeyasingham, D. and Hicks, S. (2013) The social work of sexuality: rethinking approaches to social work education. *Health and Social Care Education*, 2(2): 16–19.

Park, Y. (2005) Culture as deficit: a critical discourse analysis of the concept of culture in contemporary social work discourse, *Journal of Sociology and Social Welfare*, 32(3):11–33.

Pon, G. (2009) Cultural competency as new racism: an ontology of forgetting. *Journal of Progressive Human Services*, 20(1): 59–71.

Sakamoto, I. (2007) An anti-oppressive approach to cultural competence. *Canadian Social Work Review/Revue Canadienne de ServiceSocial*, 24(1): 105–114.

Skills for Care (2013) *Common Core Strategic Equality and Diversity Principles October 2013*. Leeds: Skills for Care.

Sundar, P. and Ly, M. (2013) Multiculturalism. In M. Gray and S. Webb (eds) *Social Work Theories and Methods* (2nd edn). London: Sage.

Taylor, C. (2003) Narrating practice: reflective accounts and the textual construction of reality. *Journal of Advanced Nursing*, 42(3): 244–251.

Thompson, N. (2012) *Anti-discriminatory Practice (5th edn)*. Basingstoke: Palgrave Macmillan.

Yee, J.Y. and Dumbrill, G. (2003) Whiteout: looking for race in Canadian social work practice. In A. Al-Krenawi and J. R. Graham (eds) *Multicultural Social Work in Canada* (pp. 98–121). Don Mills, ON: Oxford University Press.

3

YOUNG PEOPLE AS CARERS AND YOUNG USERS OF MENTAL HEALTH SERVICES: FROM POLICY TO PRACTICE

Sue McAndrew and Tony Warne

Chapter overview: **key messages**

- The psychological well-being of young people who use mental health services and young people who have taken on a caring role is an important area of concern for a contemporary health and social care agenda.
- There is an increased prevalence of mental illness among young people.
- Young carers are a particularly vulnerable group in terms of their mental health being compromised through the complex nature of taking on a caring role.
- While the adult service user and carer movement continues to grow in strength, we need to ensure the voice of the young service user and carer is given equivalence.
- Barriers to promoting better mental health for young service users and young carers need to be carefully considered and effectively addressed.
- Although policy and guidance relating to good practice exists, there is a need for organisations to promote inclusion by ensuring young people's ideas and views are heard, respected, valued and used in the development and provision of contemporary health and social care.

Introduction

This chapter aims to explore the involvement of young users of mental health services and young carers in research, education and practice within the health and social care arenas. It is specifically focused on mental health and well-being with regard to these two groups of young people, as those who experience mental illness and/or those who are caring for someone with a mental illness continue to be stigmatised (Corrigan et al., 2012; Singleton and Fry, 2015). Stigma can be thought of as being personal, public and professional. There have been a number of initiatives such as Time To Change (TTC) (Mind, 2009) and its associated strategy aimed at reducing stigma, 'Education Not Discrimination

(END)', a training programme aimed specifically to reduce mental health stigma among professionals, was also recently introduced in England. While such initiatives are aimed at reducing mental health stigma per se, young users of mental health services and those young people who are caring for a person diagnosed with mental illness are particularly vulnerable to marginalisation and exclusion (Office of Deputy Prime Minister (ODPM), 2004; Butler and Astbury, 2005; Child and Adolescent Mental Health Services (CAMHS) Review, 2008; Welsh Audit Office, 2009) impacting on their mental well-being, education, social interactions and future prospects (Banks et al., 2002; Patel et al., 2007).

Young people and mental health problems

Globally, poor mental health in young people has been attributed to a number of psychosocial factors including physical and sexual abuse, bereavement and poor family relationships, with such difficulties often being exacerbated by lower educational achievement, substance misuse, conduct problems and, due to stigma, keeping the problem hidden (Molnár et al., 2001; Patel et al., 2007; Fallon et al., 2012). Evidence suggests that half of all adults diagnosed with a mental illness had experienced their first signs and symptoms by the age of 14 years old (Patel et al., 2007). Likewise, it is estimated that 10 per cent of children and young people aged 5–16 years old have a mental health problem. Currently there are 7.5 million children and young people within this age group living in the UK, a prevalence of 9.6 per cent. It can therefore be extrapolated that 720,000 5–16 year olds will be experiencing a mental health problem (Khan et al., 2015). While it is suggested that many of these problems originate within a psychosocial domain, they are manifest as being a diagnosable illness. For example, anxiety disorders are the most common childhood psychiatric conditions, occurring in 2.2 per cent of 5–10 year olds and 4.4 per cent of 11–16 year olds, prevalence being higher among girls than boys (Green et al., 2005).

Depression is a recognised problem within adolescence, affecting 1.4 per cent of all those aged 11–16, with twice as many girls as boys said to be affected (Green et al., 2005). Children who experience depression are much more likely than other children to be from disadvantaged backgrounds, with more than 95 per cent of major depressive episodes in young people arising in those with long-term psychosocial difficulties such as parental divorce, domestic violence, abuse and school difficulties (National Institute for Clinical Excellence (NICE), 2005). In addition to depression and anxiety, admission rates for young people self-harming have risen by 68 per cent during the last decade, with recognition being given to this being the tip of the iceberg as many youngsters do not come to the attention of services (Hawton et al., 2012; McAndrew and Warne, 2014). Self-harm is most prevalent in the 11–25 year age group and a predictor of suicide, with 0.5–1 per cent of those admitted to hospital for self-harm dying by suicide within the subsequent year (Hill et al., 2011; Hawton et al., 2012). While approximately just under one third of these children and young people are able to access help, it is estimated that 500,000 do not have their mental health problems recognised and/or appropriately treated (Children's Society, 2008).

Young carers

Young carers, those providing care under the age of 18, are a global phenomenon (Robson, 2004; Becker, 2007; Moore, 2007). In England and Wales there are just under 178,000 5–17 year olds identified as young carers, 54 per cent of these being girls and 46 per cent boys (Office for National Statistics (ONS), 2013). Many of these young people are caring for a close relative (parent, sibling) who has a long-term health problem and/or is disabled. Additionally, more than half of these young carers are living in a single parent family situation, often having to take on the burden of responsibility for other family members (Dearden and Becker, 2004; McAndrew et al., 2012).

In addition to those young people who access services regarding their mental well-being, it has also been identified that over and above 'normal' adolescent difficulties, young carers have significant problems and worries that are likely to compromise their mental health (Cree, 2003). Of the 178,000 young carers, between one-third and two-thirds will be providing care for a parent who has a mental illness, which is likely to lead to them experiencing their own mental health difficulties (SCIE, 2009). As noted above there is still considerable stigma attached to mental illness in society. High levels of secrecy and shame can often be experienced when someone in the family has a mental health problem thus further complicating assessing the prevalence of young carers (Tanner, 2000; Shifren and Kachorek, 2003; ODPM, 2004).

Reflection

Think about a 14 year old having to care 24/7 for their mother who has mental health problems. List the ways in which their having to provide such care might impact on their own life.

There can be reluctance on the part of young carers to draw attention to their role for fear of being separated from their parent, negative impact on their family, or fear of being ridiculed by peers and/or being excluded from school (Princess Royal Trust, 1999; Banks et al., 2002). While some of these young people may be vulnerable to damaging and distressing situations, others harbour genuine fears that they may inherit some of the psychological problems experienced by their parent (Cooklin, 2010).

Synopsis of the adult service user and carer movement

Since the mid-1990s service user and carer engagement in health and social care practice, education and research has gathered momentum (McKeown et al., 2012; McAndrew et al., 2014). For the past two decades the involvement of service users and carers has been a central tenet of UK governments' modernisation programmes for public services (Department of Health, 2003; 2005), with service user and carer experience and knowledge recognised as key to a patient-led NHS (Warne et al., 2007; Warne and McAndrew, 2004; 2010). Consequently, many higher education institutions now incorporate service user and carer perspectives into their programmes of education and research agendas, particularly those situated in health and social care academia.

Service user and carer experience should be the lynchpin for providing quality health and social care (Warne and McAndrew, 2004; Wallcraft et al., 2011). While theoretical knowledge can provide a framework for guiding professional practice, using patient and carer experience knowledge enables professionals to contextualise theoretical concepts that often become obscured when enmeshed with everyday practice. However, service user and carer knowledge has been slow to be recognised, with many health and social care professionals continuing to believe that 'they know best'. The notion of professional knowledge being superior stems from the power imbalance inherent in the relationship between service user and professional or carer and professional (Wilkinson and McAndrew, 2008). Coming from a mental health background we are very aware of the power imbalance that exists between service user/carer/professional, the former two seeking the knowledge held by the latter. One effective way of addressing such power imbalance is to actively involve service users and carers in education, research and practice, the very processes that shape the planning, delivery and evaluation of health and social care.

Extending the movement to young people

In recent years, the adult service user and carer movement has effectively engaged in service planning, delivery and evaluation; professional education; and health and social care research agendas. However, this is not the case for young service users and carers. Similarly, while the literature focusing on adult service user and carer involvement gathers momentum, the literature relating to young service users and carers remains limited. Although policy often indicates both the desire and need to increase opportunities for children and young people to have their voices heard within the health and social care services they are likely to access (Department of Health and Department for Education and Skills,

2004; Social Care Institute for Excellence (SCIE) 2009), involving them in a similar way to adults appears to be a much slower process (Fallon et al., 2012).

Reflection

If available evidence is able to highlight the benefits of adult service user and carer involvement, consider the ways in which extending this involvement to children (5–11 year olds) and young people (11–16 year olds) might be of value.

The lack of authentic involvement of children and young people to the same extent as adult involvement is problematic. The mental health of young people is a major public health concern, not just in terms of the absence of mental illness, but also in promoting the presence of positive mental well-being. In the UK the views of young mental health service users, and their active participation in their own care, is now welcomed, with empowerment being considered as fundamental to successful service delivery, improving both the effectiveness and quality of care. Integral to empowerment is good communication, with 'being listened to' being pivotal for young people to feel respected and understood.

During the last decade there has been an increased emphasis on addressing the needs of young people who experience mental health problems (Young Minds, 2003; DoH, 2004). However, despite some acknowledgment of the importance of hearing this client group and engaging them as partners in their care, there is concern that many young people continue to find themselves nothing more than passive recipients in this process (CAMHS Review, 2008; Pryjma-chuk et al., 2014). In an earlier attempt to redress this situation some services, particularly CAMHS, have advocated empowerment as key to the delivery of successful service provision (DoH, 2004; DfES, 2006). Empowerment is considered central to improving the effectiveness and quality of mental health-care. The process of empowerment involves providing the tools and knowledge that will enable a person to take charge of their life, through making informed choices and decisions. Indeed, one of the fundamental principles of personal empowerment is control and choice related to treatment options, and this requires service providers to ensure service users have access to a variety of strategies and knowledge that will enable them to exercise such choice.

When working with young people, promoting a sense of empowerment and unconditional acceptance is particularly pertinent, but it can prove a complex task as it is often set against a backdrop of age-related transition, given that adolescence is also a time when young people are developing independence, forging their self- identity and establishing important interpersonal relationships (Coleman, 2011). Promoting empowerment requires professionals not only to have theoretical knowledge, but also knowledge of self, a level of awareness regarding their personal attributes and skills that can be utilised in the development of positive interpersonal relationships. A recent review of children and young people's views of health professionals in England (Robinson, 2010) identified a range of attributes and skills that children and young people want health professionals to possess. Communication and related issues were fundamental. These included professionals being familiar, available, accepting, informed and informative, empathic and able to ensure privacy and dignity. The importance of health and social care professionals having such personal attributes and skills in order to work effectively with children and young people has been highlighted by others (Sinclair et al., 2012; McAndrew and Warne, 2014). Clearly, as stated above, good communication and being listened to are essential if young people are to feel respected and understood and to ultimately have a sense of being empowered as active partners in care planning, delivery and evaluation.

The nuances of involving young people in education, practice and research

Young people's participation in the UK is varied and disparate, perhaps in part due to the uncertainty as to how best to involve them in effecting change (Kirby et al., 2003; Sinclair, 2006). Involving young people in various aspects of health and social care can be a complex process and one that should not be entered into lightly. Young people are a heterogeneous group and because of this it is important to match activities to the young person and/or a group of young people. Doing this will promote authenticity and a more honest, rather than tokenistic, engagement (Sinclair, 2006). In working towards achieving such involvement, careful consideration should be given as to how young people might best contribute to professional education, clinical practice and research in what can often be hierarchical organisations (McLaughlin, 2006).

Reflection
_____

Think about the ways in which the barriers to involving children and young people in professional education, practice and research could be addressed.

Although the involvement of young people in service planning and delivery is emerging as an important component for health and social care services (for example with developments such as 'Participation Works' www.participationworks. org.uk/) and research (see 'The National Young People's Mental Health Advisory Group' NIHR Clinical Research Network: Mental Health), as yet there is little available literature describing or evaluating what has been achieved to date. However, what is clear from the literature is that young people who have their expertise acknowledged can gain improved self-worth, self-esteem and ultimately confidence (Lockey et al., 2004; Fallon et al., 2012). Indeed, being listened to and taken seriously demonstrates to the young person that the expertise and strength that s/he brings to the encounter is acknowledged and valued (Lockey et al., 2004). When considering some of the research findings discussed earlier in this chapter regarding young service users and carers having poor self-esteem, low self-worth and being vulnerable to mental illness, it is important to ensure that, as professionals, we do not unconsciously add to their difficulties. Demonstrating trust and giving value to what they contribute has to be evident within the relationship if progress is to be made in developing participatory collaborative partnerships.

However, caution is required as 'listening to' and/or 'consulting' does not always equate to 'actively engaging young people' in a participatory partnership, the latter being a phenomenon more aligned to empowerment (Sinclair, 2006). To ensure active participation, adults must be mindful of the determinants that facilitate empowerment for young people. For example, the use of language, timing of meetings and equity of rights, sometimes referred to as 'ethical symmetry', are all important facets in ensuring young people experience empowerment when working in partnership with adults (Christensen and Prout, 2002; McLaughlin, 2006). Ethical symmetry, or the equity of rights between adults and young people, requires the valuing and respecting of the young person. Engagement must be a jointly negotiated process and one which acknowledges their knowledge and expertise through a shared language (Christensen and Prout, 2002). Knowledge and language are inherent in all social discourse and have the power to facilitate inclusion or exclusion (Foucault, 1972). Working to ensure the balance of power is maintained requires collaborative working between professionals and young people, effective communication and being attuned to a language that can be shared by both parties. Likewise, timing is also important. Just as adults have pressure on their time, young people also have commitments which need to be respected. While some of these will be a statutory requirement, for example, avoiding meeting times during school hours (McLaughlin, 2006), we also need to be mindful of what can sometimes be the overwhelming commitments experienced by young carers. Paying attention to language, timing and ethical symmetry will provide a platform for increased understanding, reaffirming the importance of partnership working between health and social care professionals and young people, leading to a healthy, mutually respectful working relationship (Fallon et al., 2012).

There is clearly scope for young people to help focus and prioritise the research agenda (Walderman, 2005). Young people can engage with research in a variety of ways depending on their interests, skills and experiences. For example, young people are valuable advisors about 'young person friendly language' that can be used in data collection tools, consent forms or recruitment adverts (McLaughlin, 2005; McAndrew and Warne, 2014). Likewise, young people can also act as research assistants, collecting data from their peers who may feel more at ease in speaking to another young person. When young service users and carers present research findings and, in particular, those related to their own experiences, the messages that they deliver appears to be intensified, captivating the audience (Willow et al., 2003; Rimmer and Harwood, 2004; McAndrew et al., 2012). Such contributions are thought to enhance the young person's sense of personhood and self-esteem, while at a practical level they can also add such activities to their record of achievement, thus increasing their future employability (Fallon et al., 2012).

Concerns and possible (im)practicalities

There are a number of organisational concerns and practicalities that impact on young people's involvement. Within organisations young people's participation is often seen as a complex process. If school-aged young service users and carers plan to engage in activities, statutory requirements demand the organisation register them with the local education welfare department. The department has the right to refuse consent and so great care has to be taken not to build up their hopes, as for many of them being let down may be an all too familiar feature in their lives. Likewise, young people should not be expected to walk into an organisation and immediately participate. Many of the young people discussed in this chapter will lack confidence and be unsure of their own self-worth, often being frightened to make a contribution when engaging with adult professionals who they might assume will 'know best'. It is important to bear these observations in mind even where the young person present is an apparently self-confident individual.

Reflection
___

Think about your own participation in class discussions, clinical meetings and/or research activity. Score yourself out of 10 (1: never contribute – 10: contribute all the time) and then consider what factors affect your ability to speak up or keep quiet.

For the majority of people being appropriately prepared for their involvement is vital to engage effectively. Evidence suggests that while training for adult service users and carers has grown (McKeown et al., 2012), it is not readily available for young service users and carers (Lockey et al., 2004). Lack of appropriate preparation may compromise the hopes and potential achievements of young people, and could impact negatively on their already compromised mental well-being. How an organisation will support young people in their participatory role is also important in ensuring safe practice. One suggestion to achieve this is for the young person fulfilling a participatory role to have the support of a link person from the centre where they are known, for example from Young Carers or Young Minds, who can support them by acting as a confidant, mentor and perhaps a taxi service (McLaughlin, 2006).

The issue of payment or reimbursement of any kind has been at the centre of much debate. National Children's Bureau (2003) guidelines suggest that research participants can be compensated for their time, but that this should not act as an inducement to participate. Borzekowski et al.'s (2003) poll of 127 authors found that 55 per cent had provided incentives for adolescent research participants, but that the purpose of the payment was often vague. However, the focus here is on young people as research participants, not as researchers or having involvement with other participatory roles such as educating professionals or being an active panel member for improving care services. A further ethical issue raised by Borzekowski et al., (2003), which could be applied to both being a research participant and engaging in a participatory role, was that of payment having the potential to disproportionately draw disadvantaged people to engage in situations they would not normally agree to. Although in the UK there is a minimum wage, this is age dependent, raising issues about whether all young people should receive the same amount for doing a specific role (McLaughlin, 2006). This does not necessarily equate to money, but could for example include vouchers or pre-paid tickets; however, payment does need to be agreed before they are asked to take on a role.

While the above might at times be considered obstacles to children and young people being involved in education, practice and research, overcoming them is not insurmountable. A number of articles referenced within the chapter (Willow et al., 2003; Rimmer et al., 2004; McLaughlin, 2006; Sinclair, 2006; Wilkinson and McAndrew, 2008; Fallon et al., 2012; McAndrew et al., 2012; McKeown et al., 2012) offer good examples of developing ways to overcome some of the issues raised in order to involve children and young people in education, practice and research. In addition, it might be useful to look at the following: Children's Society (2015) *The Good Childhood Inquiry: Health Research Evidence*. London: Children's Society; World Psychiatric Association's recommendations on best practices in working with service users and family carers; National Young People's Mental Health Advisory Group NIHR Clinical Research Network: Mental Health; and reports from Young Minds.

Case study: **Paulett**

Paulett is a 17 year old young woman who cares for her mother who has a long history of mental illness. During her time at high school Paulett was excluded on three occasions from two schools, due to not paying attention in class, failing to submit homework on time, absenting herself from afternoon classes and, on occasion, being verbally abusive to her teachers and peers.

Since finishing school 15 months ago Paulett has had thoughts of working in a beauty salon, but in addition to caring for her mum, she also remains the main carer for her three siblings; Ricky (10 years old), Stevie (8 years old) and Finn, who is just 5 years old.

Reflection

Based on the above information consider how Paulett's commitments at home might have impacted on her schooling.

Paulett is a quiet young woman who has low self-esteem and low self-worth. Since the age of 8 she has had bouts of low mood and harboured suicide ideation. Paulett's mental health problems have never been recognised by statutory services, despite the family having sporadic input from social workers, community mental health nurses, psychiatrists, psychologists and the family GP. Paulett admits that she never shared her suicidal thoughts with any of these people, but did, on occasion, try to explain how 'down' she was feeling.

Reflection

What factors might have caused Paulett to experience mental health problems?

Consider the reasons as to why the professionals identified above might not have picked up on Paulett's mental state.

Why might Paulett have shied away from disclosing her suicidal thoughts to those professionals visiting the family?

Approximately 18 months ago, just after being excluded from school for the final time, Paulett became aware of a local voluntary service supporting young carers. She made contact with the organisation as she was again having suicidal thoughts and worried what would happen to her siblings if she took this option. She met with a young woman, who she describes as 'kind', 'caring' and someone who 'listened to her'. After several meetings with this woman Paulett agreed to attend the support group run by the organisation for young adult carers (17–25). Paulett likes going to the group, but finds it difficult to join in the discussions.

Reflection

List the contributing factors that might have led Paulett to discuss her problems with the woman from the voluntary service.

Identify voluntary services in your own area that address issues faced by young service users and carers.

Given that for a number of purposes those 16 years and above are considered 'adult', discuss why there could be a need to recognise young adult carers as a specific group.

Paulett finds going to the group meeting a 'release'. She likes the people who attend the group and during her attendance she feels supported and no longer isolated. Paulett would like to be able to engage more fully with the group, but finds it difficult to put herself forward.

Reflection

Think about what factors might be preventing Paulett from increasing her involvement with the group.

Develop a plan of how you might encourage Paulett's involvement. Consider within the plan how you could facilitate Paulett to become empowered in taking control of her life.

In parallel to developing the plan, think about self and list your personal characteristics, skills and level of emotional intellect that would enable you to develop a relationship with Paulett that would enable your plan to successfully be put into practice.

Consider your answers to the questions above and then generate ideas how you, as a professional, could involve young service users and carers in enhancing educational programmes for professional learning, developing and improving service provision, and establishing a clear research agenda for this group of people. Think about facilitators and barriers and how you could use the former and overcome the latter.

Conclusion

As we have demonstrated, there are relatively high rates of children and young people who experience mental health problems. Whether the young person is a user of mental health services or a young carer the evidence suggests that they can both become stigmatised and marginalised and often excluded from engaging in activities. The experience of mental health problems, while often difficult and sometimes life shortening, can provide a rich reservoir of personal experience that could be harnessed and used to actively engage young people in helping to shape the health and social care services they might access. However, the involvement of children and young people in research, evaluation of services or in the educational preparation of healthcare professionals remains limited. This chapter has discussed a range of legal, ethical, emotional and psychological factors that may contribute to these low levels of involvement. While an evidence-based narrative has been developed that suggests the need to find ways of overcoming such barriers, recommended reading may initiate thinking as to how you, as a professional, might develop and enhance the process so these two groups of marginalised young people can become more effectively involved in informing and shaping future health and social care agendas.

Recommended reading

- Becker, S. (2007) Global perspective of children's unpaid caregiving in the family: research and policy on 'young carers' in the UK, Australia, the USA and Sub-Saharan Africa. *Global Social Policy,* 7(1): 23–50.

- Fallon D., Warne A., McAndrew, S. & McLaughlin H. (2012). An adult education: learning and understanding what young service users and carers really, really want in terms of their mental well being. *Nurse Education Today,* 32: 128–132.

- Khan L., Parsonage M. & Stubbs J. (2015) *Investing in Children's Mental Health: A Review of Evidence on the Costs and Benefits of Increased Service Provision.* London: Centre For Mental Health.

- National CAMHS Review (2008) *Children and Young People in Mind: Final Report of the National CAMHS Review.* London.

Relevant web links

- www.gov.uk/government/publications/the-lives-of-young-carers-in-england

- http://www.childrenssociety.org.uk/what-we-do/helping-children/young-carers?gclid=CPTynd-Nss4CFcEcGwodh84Gpg

- www.youngminds.org.uk/training_services/policy/mental_health_statistics

- www.mentalhealth.org.uk/a-to-z/c/children-and-young-people

References

Banks, P., Cogan, N., Riddell, S., Deeley, S., Hill, M. and Tisdall, K. (2002) Does the covert nature of caring prohibit the development of effective services for young carers? *British Journal of Guidance and Counselling,* 30(3): 229–246.

Becker, S. (2007) Global perspective of children's unpaid caregiving in the family: Research and policy on 'young carers' in the UK, Australia, the USA and Sub-Saharan Africa. *Global Social Policy,* 7(1): 23–50.

Borzekowski, D.L., Vaughn, E.D., Fortenberry, J.D. and Rickert, I. (2003) At what price? The current state of subject payment in adolescent research *Journal of Adolescent Health,* 33: 378–384.

Butler, A. and Astbury, G. (2005) The caring child: an evaluative case study Cornwall. Young Carers Project. *Children's Society,* 19: 292–303.

Children's Society (2008) *The Good Childhood Inquiry: Health Research Evidence.* London: Children's Society.

Christensen, P. and Prout A. (2002) Working with ethical symmetry in social research with children. *Childhood,* 9(4): 477–497.

Coleman, J.C. (2011) *The Nature of Adolescence* (4th edn). London: Routledge.

Cree, V.E. (2003) Worries and problems of young carers: issues for mental health. *Child and Family Social Work,* 8: 301–309.

Cooklin, A. (2010) Living upside down: being a young carer of a parent with mental illness. *Advances in Psychiatric Treatment,* 16: 141–146.

Corrigan, P.W., Morris, S.B., Michaels, P.J., Rafacz, J.D. and Rüsch, N. (2012) Challenging the public stigma of mental illness: a meta-analysis of outcome studies. *Psychiatric Services,* 63(10): 963–973.

Dearden, C. and Becker, S. (2004) *Young Carers in the UK.* London: The Children's Society.

Department of Health (2003) *Building on the Best; Choice Responsiveness and Equity in the NHS.* London: The Stationary Office.

_____(2004) *National Service Framework for Children, Young People and Maternity Services. The Mental Health and Psychological Wellbeing of Children and Young People.* London: HMSO.

_____(2005) *Commissioning a Patient-Led NHS.* London: The Stationary Office.

Department of Health and Department for Education and Skills (2004) *National Service Framework for Children, Young People and Maternity Services: Executive Summary.* London: Department of Health.

Fallon, D., Warne, A., McAndrew, S. and McLaughlin, H. (2012) An adult education: learning and understanding what young service users and carers really, really want in terms of their mental well being. *Nurse Education Today,* 32: 128–132.

Foucault, M. (1972) *The Archaeology of Knowledge.* London: Routledge.

Green, H., McGinnity, A., Meltzer, H., Ford, T. and Goodman, R. (2005) *Mental Health of Children and Young People in Great Britain, 2004.* London: Palgrave Macmillan.

Hawton, K., Saunders, K. and O'Connor, R. (2012) Self-harm and suicide in adolescents. *The Lancet,* 379: 2373–2382.

Hill, R., Castellanos, D. and Pettit, J. (2011) Suicide-related behaviors and anxiety in children and adolescents: a review. *Clinical Psychology Review,* 31(7): 1133–1144.

Khan, L., Parsonage, M. and Stubbs, J. (2015) *Investing in Children's Mental Health: A Review of Evidence on the Costs and Benefits of Increased Service Provision.* London: Centre for Mental Health.

Kirby, P., Lanyon, C., Cronin, K. and Sinclair, R. (2003) *Building a Culture of Participation: Involving Children and Young People in Policy, Service Planning, Development and Evaluation: A Research Report.* London: Department of Education and Skills.

Lockey, R., Sitzia, J., Gillingham, T. et al. (2004) *Training for Service Users Involvement in Health and Social Care Research: A Study of Training Provision and Participants Experiences.* Eastleigh: Involve.

McAndrew, S., Warne, A., Fallon, D. and Moran, P. (2012) Young, gifted and caring: a project narrative of young carers, their mental health and getting them involved in education, research and practice. *International Journal of Mental Health Nursing* 21: 12–19.

McAndrew, S. and Warne, T. (2014) Hearing the voices of young people who self-harm: implications for service providers. *International Journal of Mental Health Nursing,* 23(6): 570–579.

McAndrew, S., Chambers, M., Nolan, F., Thomas, B. and Watts, P. (2014) Measuring the evidence: reviewing the literature of the measurement of therapeutic engagement in acute mental health inpatient wards. *International Journal Mental Health Nursing,* 23(3): 212–220.

McKeown, M., Malihi-Shoja, L., Hogarth, R., Jones, F., Holt, K., Sullivan, P. and Mather, M. (2012) The value of involvement from the perspective of service users and carers engaged in practitioner education: not just a cash nexus. *Nurse Education Today,* 32(2): 178–184.

McLaughlin H. (2005) Young service users as co-researchers. *Qualitative Social Work,* 4(2): 21–28.

_____(2006) Involving young service users as co-researchers: possible benefits and costs. *British Journal of Social Work,* 1395–1410.

Milne, A. and Larkin, M. (2015). Knowledge generation about care-giving in the UK: a critical review of research paradigms. *Health and Social Care in the Community,* 23(1): 4–13.

Molnár, B.E., Berkman, L.F. and Buka, S.L. (2001) Psychopathology, childhood sexual abuse and other childhood adversities: relative links to subsequent suicidal behaviour in the US. *Psychological Medicine,* 31: 965–977.

Moore, T. (2007) We're all in it together: supporting young carers and their families in Australia. *Health and Social Care in the Community,* 15(6): 561–568.

National CAMHS Review (2008) Children and young people in mind: Final report of the National CAMHS review. London.

National Children's Bureau (2003) *Guidelines for Research.* London: National Children's Bureau.

NICE (2005) *Depression in children and young people: identification and management in primary, community and secondary care.* Available at: www.nice.org.uk/guidance/cg28 (accessed 29 June 2016).

Office of the Deputy Prime Minister (ODPM) (2004) *Mental Health and Social Exclusion. Social Exclusion Unit Report.* London: ODPM.

Office for National Statistics (2013) *April 2011 Census: Informed care.* London: TSO.

Patel, V., Flisher, A.J., Hetrick, S. and McGorry, P. (2007) Mental health of young people: a global public health challenge. *The Lancet,* 369: 1302–1313.

Princess Royal Trust For Carers (1999) *Too Much To Take On: a Report on Young Carers and Bullying.* London: The Princess Royal Trust for Carers.

Pryjmachuk, S., Elvey, R., Kirk, S., Kendal, S., Bower, P. and Catchpole, R. (2014) Developing a model of mental health self-care support for children and young people through an integrated evaluation of available types of provision involving systematic review, meta-analysis and case study. *Health Services and Delivery Research,* 2(18).

Rimmer, C.Y.A. and Harwood, K. (2004) Citizen participation in the education and training of social workers. *Social Work Education,* 23(3): 309–323.

Robson, E. (2004), Hidden child workers: young carers in Zimbabwe. *Antipode,* 227–248.

Robinson, S. (2010). Children and young people's views of health professionals in England. *Journal of Child Health Care,* 14(4): 310–326.

Shifren, K. and Kachorek, L.V. (2003) Does early care giving matter? The effects on young caregivers' adult mental health. *International Journal of Behavioural Development,* 27(4): 338–346.

Sinclair, R. (2006) Participation in practice: making it meaningful, effective and sustainable. *Children and Society,* 18(2): 106–118.

Sinclair, W., Camps, L. and Bibi, F. (2012) Looking after children and young people: ensuring their voices are heard in the pre-registration nursing curriculum. *Nurse Education in Practice,* doi:10.1016/j.nepr.2012.03.001.

Singleton, B.E. and Fry, G. (2015) Citizen carer: carer's allowance and conceptualisations of UK citizenship. *Journal of Social Policy,* 1–18.

Social Care Institute for Excellence (2009) *Think Child, Think Parent, Think Family: A Guide to Parental Mental Health and Child Welfare.* London: SCIE

Tanner, D. (2000) Crossing bridges over troubled waters?: Working with children of parents experiencing mental distress. *Social Work Education,* 19: 287–297.

Wallcraft, J. A. N., Amering, M., Freidin, J., Davar, B., Froggatt, D., Jafri, H. and Herrman, H. (2011) Partnerships for better mental health worldwide: WPA recommendations on best practices in working with service users and family carers. *World Psychiatry,* 10(3): 229–236.

Warne, T., McAndrew S., King M. and Holland K., (2007) Rhetorical organisations of defense in primary care. *Primacy Health Care Research and Development,* 8(2): 183–192.

Warne T. and McAndrew S. (eds) (2004) *Using Patient Experience in Nurse Education.* Basingstoke: Palgrave.

_____(eds) (2010) *Creative Approaches in Health and Social Care Education and Practice: Knowing Me, Understanding You.* Basingstoke: Palgrave.

Wearing, M. (2011) Strengthening youth citizenship and social inclusion practice—The Australian case: Towards rights based and inclusive practice in services for marginalized young people. *Children and Youth Services Review,* 33(4): 534–540.

Welsh Audit Office (2009) *Services for Children and Young People with Emotional and Mental Health Needs.* Wales.

Wilkinson, C. and McAndrew, S. (2008) 'I'm not an outsider, I'm his mother!' A phenomenological enquiry into carer experiences of exclusion from acute psychiatric settings. *International Journal of Mental Health Nursing,* 17: 392–401.

Willow, C., Marchant, R., Kirby, P. and Neale, B. (2003) *Citizenship for Young Children: Strategies for Development.* York: Joseph Rowntree Foundation.

Young Minds Organisation (2003) *Where Next? New Directions in In-Patient Mental Health Services for Young People.* London: Young Minds Organisation.

4

MARGINALISED CHILDREN AND YOUNG PEOPLE WITH AUTISM SPECTRUM DISORDERS

Andrea Brammer, Rob Kennedy and Frances Binns

Chapter overview: **key messages**

- The major challenges for children and young people with autism spectrum disorders relate to social interactions with people and the environment. These challenges are brought into sharp focus when the child/young person requires healthcare intervention.
- Collaborative working is necessary to improve the patient experience and quality of services for children and young people with autism.
- Reasonable adjustments enable access and inclusion in children's health services and are complemented by multi-agency collaboration in order to ensure successful clinical outcomes.

Introduction

Autism is a spectrum of developmental disorders characterised by deficits in verbal and emotional communication, social reciprocal interaction with stereo-typed, repetitive, or unusual behaviours or interests (Inglese, 2009; Levy et al., 2010). Autism is referred to as a *spectrum* of disorders due to the way in which its manifestations can occur in a variety of combinations and be present in varying degrees of severity (Inglese, 2009). Although the term autism will be used in this chapter, it also refers to children and young people with Asperger's Syndrome, Pervasive Developmental Disorder and learning disabilities as there appears to be a strong correlation between learning disability and co-morbidity occurring as autism. Although there is a dearth of specific data, it appears that children with learning disabilities may also have a reduced ability to under-stand new and complex information (DH, 2009). This inability to comprehend complex information is related to limited language skills which reduces the child's ability to report their symptoms or distress, which may be manifested as challenging behaviours (MENCAP, 2004). Autism is an increasingly recognised condition and it is suggested that 1–2 per cent of the primary school-aged population in the United Kingdom may be affected (Baron-Cohen et al., 2009).

In meeting the needs of children and young people and their families, it is recognised that inequalities in distribution of resources limit the holistic care and development of treatment and support strategies available for children and young people, as well as adults, with Autism Spectrum Disorders (ASD). Evidence indicates that this results in patients with and without a diagnosis of ASD having unmet needs (National Autistic Society, 2014; Kennedy and Binns, 2014; NICE, 2013, 2014). In this chapter we explore the complexities of meeting the personalised care for a child or young person with a diagnosis of autism. To place this into context, a child's journey using a 'virtual' Radiology Department, focusing upon the patient/family journey, will highlight the inequalities of this group of patients.

The global context

A plethora of literature suggests that the prevalence of ASD continues to increase across the world in the second decade of the twenty-first century (Chiri and Warfield, 2012; Baron-Cohen et al., 2009) with an estimated rate of 1 in 63 being reported in the United Kingdom (UK) (Baron-Cohen et al., 2009). The ratio of individuals with ASD is reported to be 7:1 male to female (Whiteley et al., 2010) and this is anecdotally experienced in clinical practice. The implication of this increase in diagnosis is that young people (and their families) have a definitive diagnosis of the condition that they are living with, but they have limited access to appropriate support and treatment to help them to understand and manage the condition (Baron-Cohen et al., 2009; Couteur et al., 2008). An increase in prevalence of ASD therefore equates to an increase in required resources and associated costs to meet the increased needs (Briggs, 2014); yet the cost of heart disease, stroke and cancer combined is less than the health costs of ASD (London School of Economics and Political Science, 2014). Conversely, the amount of money committed to research for ASD is insignificant in comparison (£6.60 per person with ASD compared with £295 per person with cancer). In the current economic climate, with dwindling, pressurised resources available, it can perhaps be seen how inequalities in health become manifest.

Children and young people with autism have a range of symptoms, including experiencing increased levels of stress and distress when exposed to highly stimulating situations (Aylott, 2010; Kopecky et al., 2013). This affects the way in which a child and young person interacts with their surroundings and other people (National Autistic Society, 2014). Prior to the National Service Framework (NSF) 2003 for Autism, children and young people who were suspected of having ASD received fragmented diagnosis and minimal intervention following their diagnosis, let alone continued support. This historically led to children and young people being labelled as 'the naughty child' (Brownson, 2014), due to a lack of multi professional and societal understanding, leading to inequitable delivery of care and support.

Reflection

Consider a child or young person that you have come into contact with; think about how they communicate and interact with the world around them. Consider how a child with a diagnosis of autism might interact. Do you think that this would impact upon your ability to communicate with them?

Associated comorbidities of ASD and medical interventions

Evidence from literature demonstrates the increase in ASD when the associated comorbidities children and young people with ASD report are taken into consideration: for example, sleep problems, epilepsy, gastro intestinal problems, endocrine and many others (Parellada et al., 2013; Tregnago and Cheak-Zamora, 2012; Goulston et al., 2009; Chiri and Warfield, 2012). With the current estimate of 1 in 63 children and adults having ASD, and the subsequent increase in referrals for medical intervention and support, healthcare professionals are increasingly likely to work with children and young people and/or parent and carers with ASD. It is evident that this client group of children, young people and adults is increasing, and therefore there will be an impact upon the delivery of healthcare.

Challenging behaviour may be the only indicator of a medical problem in a child or young person with ASD and this behaviour may not directly correlate with the medical situation (Parellada et al., 2013; Carr and Owen-DeSchryver, 2007). For example, for a child or young person/parent with ASD who does not communicate verbally, identifying the source of a clinical problem is a significant issue. It is therefore imperative that healthcare professionals listen to children, young people and their families who invariably spend a considerable amount of time with their children and are 'experts' in recognising their child's behaviour patterns (Scarpinato et al., 2010).

Economic impact and resources

Children, young people and adults with ASD frequently have comorbidities associated with the spectrum, such as gastrointestinal, ophthalmological, endocrine, epilepsy, mental health and neurology problems (Bultas, 2012; O'Reilly, 2014), resulting in increased demand for healthcare and adding to the financial pressure placed upon the National Health Service and other supporting organisations. Healthcare is defined as 'benefits from health education, disease prevention, diagnosis, treatment, rehabilitation and terminal care' (Wright, Williams and Wilkinson, 1998: 1310). As a result, services for children and adults with ASD cost more than several prominent diseases combined; yet proportionally ASD receives a small fraction in funding for research (Briggs, 2014).

Equality in accessing healthcare

Failure to overcome barriers and provide reasonable adjustments for children and young people with ASD equates to discrimination (Hebron, 2011). Evidence indicates the failure of organisations to make adjustments (Bultas, 2012; Goulston et al., 2009) and suggests that it is still not routine practice in the UK to develop reasonable adjustments for patients with ASD despite it being a legal requirement (The National Autistic Society, 2013). The Autism Act (2009) stipulates that healthcare staff working with adult patients with ASD should have specialist training about ASD; it is possible that children are not specified as it is assumed that paediatric teams already have the knowledge and experience to deal with these patients (Walsh and Hall, 2012). The Equality Act (2010) states that public services should make 'reasonable adjustments' for disabled patients in order to improve their care. In addition, several recent reports have highlighted poor practice for vulnerable patients, and have placed responsibility on public sector services to improve quality and patient safety (DoH, 2012; Francis, 2013; Berwick, 2013; Keogh, 2013). These reports state that patients should be involved in decision making about their care.

Healthcare workers in the National Health Service (NHS) have an ethical obligation to look after patients with ASD, yet reports published such as the Department of Health's report into Winterbourne View Hospital unfortunately illustrate that this is not always the case (DoH, 2012). Nevertheless, the media frequently report high-profile cases where patients are not receiving the (basic) care that they are entitled to (ITV plc, 2014). Children, young people and adults with ASD are eligible for the same healthcare that the rest of the population is entitled to (Autism Act, 2009; Equality Act, 2010; Health and Social Care Act, 2012). Failure to provide appropriate healthcare to this cohort of patients may amount to discrimination (Autism Act, 2009) and may result in patients having delayed or missed diagnosis which negatively impacts on health outcomes (Rhoades, Scarpa and Salley, 2007).

Brammer (2015) highlights that physicians do not listen to patients' needs (Carbone et al., 2010; Bultas, 2012). Failure to listen to the needs of patients with ASD may result in the patient exhibiting challenging behaviour, which in turn may negatively affect the clinical outcome of an investigation or treatment (Van Der Valt and Moran, 2001; Kopecky et al., 2013). Several reports have been published which emphasise to healthcare staff the importance of listening to patients and their carers in a bid to improve not only quality of care delivered to patients but also patient safety (Berwick, 2013; Francis, 2013; Keogh, 2013). Children, young people and adults with ASD have more unmet health needs than the rest of the population (Shieve et al., 2012; Tregnago and Cheak-Zamora, 2012; Chiri and Warfield, 2012). Chiri and Warfield (2012) described unmet needs in the following healthcare services:

- Routine preventative care;
- Specialist care;
- Physical, occupational or speech therapy;
- Mental healthcare or counselling.

Research findings demonstrate that there are unmet needs in relation to supporting families with financial problems (Shieve et al., 2012; Tregnago and Cheak-Zamora, 2012). All of these findings originated in the United States; however, these may be transferable to the United Kingdom population and consist of:

1. low family income or inability to meet the cost of specialist care (Shieve et al., 2012; Tregnago and Cheak-Zamora, 2012) (this phenomenon is unlikely to be reported in the UK due to the NHS and subsequent 'free' provision of services);
2. a delay in care (Shieve et al., 2012; Tregnago and Cheak-Zamora, 2012). This is likely to be reported in the UK due to barriers accessing healthcare.

In the UK it is recognised that 'hard to reach' groups such as homeless people, travellers or refugees (Pfeil and Howe, 2004) exist and frequently do not receive equitable access to healthcare due the very nature of their background.

Barriers to health and diagnostic treatment

Research findings demonstrate that children, young people and their families with ASD reported difficulty accessing healthcare (Parellada et al., 2013; Tregnago and Cheak-Zamora, 2012; Bultas, 2012; Chiri and Warfield, 2012). There are a variety of factors described which contribute to this difficulty:

- Failure to make reasonable adjustments (Parellada et al., 2013; Tregnago and Cheak-Zamora, 2012).

- Communication difficulties (Parellada et al., 2013).

- Lack of expertise of clinicians (Parellada et al., 2013; Tregnago and Cheak-Zamora, 2012).

In addition to those noted above, barriers to healthcare (Parellada et al., 2013) may include:

- long waiting times;

- over stimulating environment;

- high out of pocket expenses/low income;

- lack of time/timing of appointments;

- child's behaviour/characteristics of ASD;

- bureaucracy/referral problems/rigidity.

Evidently, accessing routine healthcare treatment can often be complex, challenging, ineffective and costly for the child or young person with ASD. For example, accessing diagnostic images in a Radiology Department relies upon cooperation of the child and support from their family/carers. However, for many children and young people with ASD, the actual process can be fraught (Brammer, 2015). When arriving at the Radiology Department multi-sensory problems may trigger challenging behaviour, including normal everyday situations such as leaving home, getting in a car and visiting an unfamiliar place. When the child with ASD has arrived in the Radiology Department they may then be required to change into a hospital gown. Many children and young people with ASD find the movement of clothes across the surface of their skin to be very sensitive and this may also become a barrier to a successful radiology experience (Grandin, 2006).

Goulston et al. (2009) specifically explored issues within the radiology environment and concluded that in addition to barriers already described, the following phenomena are present:

- Separation anxiety (the patient is asked to enter the examination room without their parent/carer);

- Inadequate information essential for preparing the child and young person to be separated from their parent/carer;

- Staff attitudes (including lack of understanding of the child's needs, lack of care, 'controlling parent' behaviour of healthcare professionals – encourages anxiety in the child; anticipatory fear of dealing with challenging behaviour).

Goulston et al. (2009) suggest that these problems can be overcome with improved communication with the child and their parent/carer and also with carefully planned preparation. Lai et al. (2012) suggest that all healthcare professionals should have an awareness of ASD as determined by the Autism Act (2009) (Kennedy and Binns, 2014). Within the specific setting of the radiology department, children and young people who are unable to tolerate radiology imaging have the following options:

- Do not have a diagnostic test (Lyon and Reeves, 2006a).

- Immobilisation for the imaging procedure (The Society of Radiographers, 2012).

- Referral for therapeutic safe holding, sedation or general anaesthetic (chemical restraint) (Nordahl et al., 2008; Khan et al., 2007; Kennedy and Binns, 2016).

- Hospital Play Specialists (HPS) utilised to enable cooperation (Kennedy and Binns, 2016).

Reasonable adjustments

It is difficult to find a decisive description of 'reasonable adjustments'. However, Atkinson (2011) discusses the implications of the Equality Act 2010, the Health and Social Care Act 2012 and the Autism Act 2009 in conjunction with recommendations made in the report 'Healthcare for All' (Michael, 2008) and clearly summarises what constitutes a 'reasonable adjustment'. In many respects, making reasonable adjustments requires a simple and straightforward approach, placing the child and young person and their family at the centre of everything. It is about them, their child's treatment and how the organisation, or in the case study utilised in this chapter the Radiology Department, can fit in around them and meet their individualised specific needs, not how they 'must' fit in to departmental ways of working that are often process driven and based upon historical, outdated methods of care delivery.

Atkinson (2011) considers that enhancing co-ordination of healthcare by supporting the use of locally agreed portable portfolios, or 'health passports', which contain a brief outline of a person's health issues and history and which people with learning disabilities can take to healthcare appointments will help in planning, communication and flexibility of care delivery while also ensuring that healthcare staff understand and apply the principles of mental capacity legislation, including how to promote informed decision making, as well as how to make a decision in a person's best interests when they cannot make their own choices. The availability of autism/learning disability liaison nurses, who support service users, carers and healthcare staff through communication, coordination and the application of specialist knowledge when children and young people attend acute hospitals, is key to this. Part of the nurse specialist role would also be to ensure that children and young people can access annual health checks within primary care; awareness training for all staff in healthcare services; providing practical support and information to families and carers and providing information regarding services, health conditions, treatments and important health promotion messages in formats that are more accessible for children and young people with ASD and/or a learning disability; this could include the use of pictures, symbols, easy to follow language and DVDs.

Reasonable adjustments to support equitable access to healthcare

Some barriers could potentially be overcome by making 'reasonable adjustments' to accommodate children and young people with ASD. For example:

- **Bureaucracy** could be reduced by improving communication between parents and healthcare providers, planning ahead and by the use of social stories (Aylott, 2010).

- **Patient condition** issues could be improved by adapting communication methods to suit the child with ASD; listening to parents/carers as to what their childs 'do's and don'ts' are (Aylott, 2010);

- **Environmental** problems could be addressed by more time for appointments, more convenient scheduling which suits the child and family, the prioritisation of children and young people with ASD to avoid lengthy waits, provision of a quite area to avoid over stimulation.

- **Healthcare profesional** problems could be improved through training, utilising 'Positive about Autism™' training and an ASD Champion model (Aylott, 2010; Kennedy and Binns, 2014; Major et al., 2013;The National Austistic Society, 2014).

The literature stating what reasonable adjustments should be made for children and young people with ASD does not clarify if these adjustments have been discussed with the patient and/or their family/carers and it can be argued that healthcare professionals have assumed what reasonable adjustments should be made. This assumption should be tested by evaluating the impact of reasonable adjustments on access to healthcare for children, young people, adults and families with ASD.

Person Centred Needs Assessments (PCNA)

Health needs assessments emerged following reforms to the NHS in the 1990s (Wright et al., 1998) as an evidence-based tool to deliver equitable and efficient healthcare being available for all, at a time when resources were becoming limited and members of the public were becoming more active in expressing their views about quality of service. Wright et al. (1998) state that identified health needs should be met with effective intervention, maintaining that there is an overlap with 'need', 'demand' and 'supply'. Health needs assessments are an opportunity to identify areas of unmet needs and to develop strategies to overcome these (Wright et al., 1998). One important aspect of health needs assessments is the epidemiology of the disease (Williams and Wright, 1998) in order to develop strategies to cope with specific ailments and many needs assessments were developed for populations of people (Wilkinson and Murray, 1998) with assessments being carried out at various levels.

In the twenty-first century, needs assessments have become more 'person centred' in their approach (National Disability Authority, 2012); identifying what actions are required in order for the child to achieve a specific goal is recognisable in the Person Centred Needs Assessment (PCNA). Discussion in 1998, surrounding PCNA, debated the dilemma of which individuals had a greater health need in order to compete for limited resources (Stevens and Gillam, 1998) and PCNAs were generally completed by medical staff to fight for individual cases, rather than to identify the quality of the hospital experience from the perspective of the child and family. Evaluation of health needs assessments to identify gaps in care was also deemed to be important (Wilkinson and Murray, 1998).

Case study 1: **David**

David, a 10 year old boy with ASD, was referred to the local hospital for radiographic exploration prior to having surgery to correct his kyphoscoliosis (curvature of the spine). His parents were both extremely anxious before attending the hospital as he had no previous experience of being an inpatient. David finds other life situations challenging due to his sensory processing disorder and limited mobility. The spinal surgeon informed David's parents during his outpatient consultation that he will require a pre-operative

➧

blood test and a further x-ray of his spine. He would also need to have a general anaesthetic for the spinal surgery.

As a healthcare practitioner, how could you:

- Prepare David and his family for his admission and diagnostic tests?
- Prepare the environment that David is in?
- How would you know that you were getting it right?

Now consider the case study below.

Case study 2: **Reflections from a member of staff involved in delivering support to a young person with autism**

Rizwan arrived at the x-ray department for his appointment with his mum, dad, sibling and myself as his care support worker. The waiting area was very busy due to the Scoliosis clinic running. Nita (Rizwan's mum) informed me that it is always a very busy clinic. I asked the radiographers at the time how long it would be before Rizwan could be seen for his x-ray. I was informed that due to the number of patients waiting and the severity of some of the cases, it would be difficult to give an estimation of the length of time that Rizwan would have to wait.

Rizwan appeared to be 'ok' for the first fifteen minutes after we arrived in the waiting area but soon became over stimulated, due to the high levels of noise and strange people. I suggested to his mother Nita that they could wait in the Ultrasound waiting area as there was nobody there, but this was going against the preparation that Rizwan had been shown, and would have upset him more. Due to the nature of the clinic and being unsure who was doing the x-rays it was difficult to be able to pass on relevant information about Rizwan's needs. I advised two of the radiographers not to speak to Rizwan as unfamiliar voices and faces often caused him to become very agitated and upset and to instruct mum what needed to happen. I also confirmed that the lights could be left on for Rizwan for his x-ray as I knew he did not like the dark.

After an hour and a half of waiting, Rizwan went into the x-ray room. I made sure that the room was as it was in the photographs Rizwan had been using; the Thomas the Tank video was also playing. Nita was anxious, as Rizwan had become over stimulated by this point, and it was going to be very difficult to get him in the room and to settle him when he was in the room.

Nita brought him down to the room; as two radiographers went into the room I waited outside the room. Rizwan was highly anxious by this point and did not want to be in the room. He attempted to bite one of the radiographers. The radiographer came out of the room after approximately 10 minutes, to allow some time for mum to try and calm Rizwan, but this was unsuccessful. Although he had approximately a 15-minute appointment, due to other patients waiting to be seen there was not the time for him to be able to acclimatise to the room. Also heightened by the length of waiting time, Rizwan's anxiety levels were too high for him to be able to take everything in.

Nita suggested that it would be appropriate for Rizwan to be able to attend the department outside the Scoliosis clinic times at a quieter time to be able to accommodate his needs. Nita felt the preparation had been a waste of time. Nita felt that it would be more difficult for him to come back as it would become a game to Rizwan; therefore, it would be more difficult to gain his co-operation for the x-ray. Afterwards Nita said that she was unhappy he could not be seen straight away and that his needs were not taken into account.

Nita made a formal complaint.

Reflection

1. Can you identify what went wrong?
2. What could have been done differently?

Transition to adult services

With increased prevalence of ASD it follows that there will be an increasing number of children and young people moving into adult services (Parellada et al., 2013; Shieve et al., 2012; Bultas, 2012; Lai et al., 2012; Chiri and Warfield, 2012). Transition into adult services is a complex and confusing process involving families (Watson et al., 2011; Colver et al., 2013) and healthcare workers in the paediatric and adult field, requiring robust strategies to deal with the process (Hamdani et al., 2011). Transition typically occurs between the ages of 16 and 18 years (Watson et al., 2011). However, there is evidence of extending this age range to between 14 and 25 years (Watson et al., 2011). Failure to transfer to adult services may result in unmet health needs (Stevenson et al., 1997; Watson, 2000; Nakhla et al., 2009; Colver et al., 2013) as there are no transition models for children and young people with ASD (Watson et al., 2011; Hamdani et al., 2011; Colver et al., 2013; Cheak-Zamora et al., 2014). There are suggestions that it should be a holistic approach (Colver et al., 2013). Paucity of transition models for children with ASD may be due to a lack of identified need and lack of availability of adult services (Department of Health, 2006b, 2010; Singh et al., 2010).

To complicate the matter of transition further, definitions of adolescence vary between 10/12–19 years (World Health Organization, 2015) and 10–19 years old (UNICEF, 2011) with additional definitions of youth and young people extending until the age of 24 (World Health Organization, 2015; UNICEF, 2011; Colver et al., 2013). Additionally, improvements in healthcare resulted in improved lifespan expectancies of children with disabilities causing an increased need for adult healthcare services as they were no longer eligible for paediatric care (Hamdani et al., 2011), which consequently led to unmet health needs.

Many healthcare providers accept children up to the age of 16 years, yet in April 2015, a paediatric surgeon at a local children's hospital divulged that he is frequently asked to accept 19 year olds as new patients for surgery due to advances in medicine resulting in patients, who a few years ago would not have been expected to survive childhood, now surviving and needing continued care. The adult teams, having not dealt with this cohort of patients, do not have the skills and competences to look after these patients. This correlates with evidence regarding lack of availability of adult services for this cohort of patients (Department of Health, 2006b, 2010; Singh et al., 2010).

Conclusion

In summary, it is unequivocal that there is an increase in the prevalence of ASD, and the associated comorbidities result in an increase in the numbers of children and young people with ASD accessing healthcare. It is also well evidenced that children and young people with ASD struggle to negotiate the healthcare environment without demonstrating challenging behaviour, and this may negatively impact on the effectiveness of their treatment. Evidence also suggests that patients with ASD have problems accessing healthcare in the first place, and have unmet needs. In order to ensure that patients with ASD are able to receive the healthcare that they are entitled to, it is necessary, and a legal requirement, to provide reasonable adjustments while at the same time complying with legislation ensuring that the rights of the patient are maintained.

It has been demonstrated that some organisations are making reasonable adjustments for children and young people with ASD and there is literature which attempts to identify how access to healthcare can be improved for those with ASD. Brammer (2015) suggests that in order to deliver clinically effective and truly inclusive healthcare for all children and young people and their families with ASD the following recommendations must be followed:

- Completion of individual needs assessment by all healthcare teams on admission to all areas of the healthcare practice.

- Implementation of personalised reasonable adjustments for children and young people with ASD.

- Provision of quiet areas for children and young adults with ASD in all settings

- Mandatory autism training for all staff working with children, young people and adults with ASD.

- Improved use of communication tools for all individuals with ASD.

- Communicating with and learning from each other locally and nationally to improve quality of care to children and young people with ASD and their families.

Anecdotal evidence (gathered through the authors' encounters in professional contexts) suggests that there remains a culture in some areas where medical staff and healthcare professionals are resistant to change practice. This would appear to challenge the assertion that children and young people's services have the knowledge and skills to deal with children and young people with ASD (Walsh and Hall, 2012).

Recommended reading

- Kennedy, R. and Binns, F. (2014) Communicating and managing children and young people with autism and extensive burn injury. *Wounds UK, 10*(3).

- Page, A., Mcdonnell, A., Gayson, C., Moss, F., Mohammed, N., Smith, C. and Vanes, N. (2015) Clinical holding with children who display behaviours that challenge. *British Journal of Nursing,* 24(21): 1086–1093.

- Vaz, I. (2013) Visual symbols in healthcare settings for children with learning disabilities and autism spectrum disorder. *British Journal of Nursing,* 22(3): 156–159.

Relevant web links

- www.autism.org.uk/

- www.positiveaboutautism.co.uk/

- www.cmft.nhs.uk/childrens-hospitals/our-services/services-for-children-with-autism

- www.cafamily.org.uk/

References

Atkinson, D.T.B. (2011) Improving health outcomes for people with learning disabilities. *Nursing Standard,* 26(6): 33–36.
Autism Act 2009. London: The Stationery Office Limited.

Aylott, J. (2010) Improving access to health and social care for people with autism. *Nursing Standard,* 24(27): 47–56.

Baron-Cohen, S., Scott, F.J., Allison, C., Williams, J., Bolton, P., Matthews, F.E., et al. (2009) Prevalence of autism-spectrum conditions: UK school-based population study. *The British Journal of Psychiatry,* 194: 500–509.

Berwick, D. (2013) *A Promise to Learn – A Commitment to Act; Improving the Safety of Patients in England.* London: Williams Lea.

Brammer. A (2015) A service evaluation of the impact of person centred needs assessments for patients with Autism-Spectrum Disorder (ASD) prior to attending the Radiology Department. University of Bolton.

Briggs, H. (2014) *Autism costs '£32bn per year' in UK.* Available at: www.bbc.co.uk/news/health-27742716?print=true (accessed 5 February 2016).

Brownson. D (2014) *He's Not Naughty! A Children's Guide to Autism.* Askam-in-Furness: Bodhi Book Press Ltd.

Carbone, P.S., Behl, D.D. and Azor, V. (2010) The Medical Home for Children with Autism Spectrum Disorder: Parent and Pediatrician Perspectives. *Journal of Autism Developmental Disorder,* 40: 317–324.

Carr, E.G. and Owen-DeSchryver, J.S. (2007) Physical illness, pain, and problem behaviour in minimally verbal people with development disabilities. *Journal of Autism Development Disorder,* 37: 413–424.

Centers for Disease Control and Prevention (2014) *National Survey of Children with Special Health Care Needs.* Available at: www.cdc.gov/nchs/slaits/cshcn.htm (accessed 8 February 2016).

Charman, T. and Gotham, K. (2013) Measurement issues: screening and diagnostic instruments for autism spectrum disorders - lessons from research and practise. *Child and Adolescent Mental Health,* 18(1): 52–64.

Cheak-Zamora, N.C., Farmer, J.E., Mayfield, W.A., Clark, M.J. and Marvin, A.R. (2014) Health care transition services for youth with autism spectrum disorders. *Rehabilitation Psychology,* 59(3): 340–348.

Chebuhar, A., McCarthy, A. M., Bosch, J., and Baker, S. (2013) Using picture schedules in medical settings for patients with an autism spectrum disorder. *Journal of Pediatric Nursing,* 28: 125–134.

Chiang, H.-M. (2008) Expressive communication of children with autism: the use of challenging behaviour. *Journal of Intellectual Disability Research,* 52(11): 966–972.

Chiri, G. and Warfield, M.E. (2012) Unmet need and problems accessing core health care services for children with autism spectrum disorder. *Maternal Child Health,* 16: 1081–1091.

Colver, A.F., Merrick, H., Deverill, M., Le Couteur, A., Parr, J., Pearce, M.S., et al. (2013) Study protocol: longitudinal study of the transition of young people with complex health needs from child to adult health services. *BMC Public Health,* 13.

Couteur, A.L., Haden, G., Hammal, D. and McConachie, H. (2008) Diagnosing autism spectrum disorders in pre-school children. *Journal of Autism Development Disorder Using Two Standardised Assessment Instruments: The ADI-R and the ADOS,* 38: 362–372.

Dearlove, O. and Corcoran, J.P. (2007) Sedation of children undergoing magnetic resonance imaging. *British Journal of Anaesthesia,* 98(4): 548–549.

Department of Health (2006a) *Better services for people with an Autistic Spectrum Disorder.* Available at: http://webarchive.nationalarchives.gov.uk/20130107105354/http://www.dh.gov.uk/prod_consum_dh/groups/dh_digitalassets/@dh/@en/documents/digitalasset/dh_065238.pdf (accessed 9 February 2016).

_____*Transition: Getting It Right for Young People.* Available at: http://webarchive.nationalarchives.gov.uk/20130107105354/http:/www.dh.gov.uk/prod_consum_dh/groups/dh_digitalassets/@dh/@en/documents/digitalasset/dh_4132149.pdf (accessed 9 February 2016).

_____(2008) *High Quality Care for All.* Available at: http://webarchive.nationalarchives.gov.uk/+/www.dh.gov.uk/en/Healthcare/Highqualitycareforall/index.htm (accessed 9 February 2016).

_____(2010) *'Fulfilling and Rewarding Lives'. The Strategy for Adults with Autism in England.* London: Department of Health.

_____(2012) *Department of Health Review: Winterbourne View Hospital Interim Report.* London: Department of Health.

_____(2012) *Winterbourne View Summary of the Government Response.* London: Department of Health.

Francis, R. (2013) *Report of the Mid Staffordshire NHS Foundation Trust Public Inquiry.* London: The Stationary Office.

Grandin, T. (2006) *Thinking in Pictures: And Other Reports from My Life with Autism* (2nd edn). London: Doubleday.

Guthrie, W., Swineford, L.B., Nottke, C. and Wetherby, A.M. (2013) Early diagnosis of autism spectrum disorder: stability and change in clinical diagnosis and symptom presentation. *The Journal of Child Psychology and Psychiatry,* 54(5): 582–590.

Hamdani, Y., Jetha, A. and Norman, C. (2011) Systems thinking perspectives applied to healthcare tranistion for youth with disabilities: a paradigm shift for practice, policy and research. *Child: Care, Health and Development,* 37(6): 806–814.

Harvey-Lloyd, J.M. (2013) Operating within the legal and ethical framework to gain co-operation when imaging paediatric patients. *Radiography,* 19: 285–289.

Health and Social Care Act (2012), c.7. London: The Stationery Office Limited.

Healthcare Commission (2007) *An improving picture? Imaging services in acute and specialist trusts.* London: Commission for Healthcare Audit and Inspection.

Hebron, C. (2011) Developing tools to enable easier access to mainstream services. *Learning Disability Practice,* 14(9): 22–26.

Inglese, M.D., (2009) Caring for children with autism spectrum disorder part ii: screening, diagnosis and management. *Journal of Pediatric Nursing,* 24:1: 49–59.

ITV Plc (2014) *Chief inspector of hospitals: Failing hospitals 'need more help'.* Available at: www.itv.com/news/granada/update/2014-08-04/chief-inspector-of-hospitals-failing-hospitals-need-more-help/ (accessed 5 February 2016).

Kahn, J.J., Lane, F.D., Koch, B.L., Curtwright, L.A., Dickerson, J.M. and Hardin, J.L. (2007) A program to decrease the need for pediatric sedation for CT and MRI. *Applied Radiology,* 36(4): 30–33.

Kennedy, R. and Binns, F. (2014) Communicating and managing children and young people with autism and extensive burn injury. *Wounds UK,* 10(3): 60–65.

Keogh, B. (2013) *Review into the Quality of Care and Treatment Provided by 14 Hospital Trusts in England: Overview Report.* Available at: www.nhs.uk/nhsengland/bruce-keogh-review/documents/outcomes/keogh-review-final-report.pdf (accessed 5 February 2016).

Kohn, C. (2014) *Sensory Overload.* Available at: http://craigkohntheaspergerscoach. blogspot.co.il/ (accessed 5 February 2016).

Kopecky, K., Broder-Fingert, S., Iannuzzi, D. and Connors, S. (2013) The needs of hospitalized patients with autism spectrum disorders: a parent survey. *Clinical Pediatrics,* 52(7): 652–660.

Lai, B., Milano, M., Roberts, M.W. and Hooper, S.R. (2012) Unmet dental needs and barriers to dental care among children with autism spectrum disorders. *Journal of Autism Development Disorder,* 42: 1294–1303.

Levy, S.E., Giarelli, E., Lee, L.C., Shieve, L.A., Kirby, R.S., Cunniff, C. and Rice, C. (2010) Autism spectrum disorder and co-occurring developmental, psychiatric and medical conditions among multiple populations of the United States. *Journal of Developmental and Behavioural Pediatrics,* 4: 267–274.

London School of Economics and Political Science. (2014) *Autism is the Most Costly Medical Condition in the UK.* Available at: www.lse.ac.uk/newsAndMedia/news/ archives/2014/06/Autism.aspx (accessed 5 February 2016).

Lyon, R. and Reeves, P.J. (2006a) An investigation into why patients do not attend for out-patient radiology appointments. *Radiography,* 12: 283–290.

Major, N.E., Peacock, G., Ruben, W., Thomas, J. and Weitzman, C.C. (2013) Autism training in pediatric residency: evaluation of a case-based curriculum. *Journal of Autism and Developmental Disorder,* 43: 1171–1177.

Manikiza, J., Jones, C., James, T. and Robinson, S. (2010) *Autistic Spectrum Disorders; Primary Healthcare Settings.* Cardiff: Welsh Assembly Government.

MedicineNet.com (2015) *Definition of Atypical.* Available at: www.medicinenet.com/ script/main/art.asp?articlekey=9825 (accessed 5 February 2016).

Memari, A.H., Ziaee, V., Mirfazeli, F.S. and Kordi, R. (2012) Investigation of autism comorbidities and associations in a school-based community sample. *Journal of Child and Adolescent Psychiatric Nursing,* 25: 84–90.

Michael, J. (2008) *Healthcare for all: Report of the Independent Inquiry into Access to Healthcare for People with Learning Disabilities.* London: Aldridge Press.

NICE (2013) *Autism in Under 19's: Support and Management.* National Institute for Clinical Excellence Guideline CG170. London: NICE.

_____(2015) *Challenging Behaviour and Learning Disabilities: Prevention and Interventions for People with Learning Disabilities whose Behaviour Challenges.* National Institute for Clinical Excellence, Guideline NG11. London: NICE.

Nakhla, M., Daneman, D., To, T., Paradis, G. and Guttman, A. (2009) Transition to adult care for youths with diabetes mellitus: findings from a universal health care system. *Pediatrics,* 124(6): 1134–1141.

National Autistic Society (2014) *Autism and Asperger Syndrome: An Introduction.* Available at: www.autism.org.uk/about/what-is.aspx (accessed 5 February 2016).

National Disability Authority (2012) *So What is 'Person Centred Planning'? Definition and Brief History.* Available at: http://nda.ie/Good-practice/Guidelines/Guidelines-on-Person-Centered-Planning/Guidelines-on-Person-Centred-Planning-format-versions/2-What-is-Person-Centred-Planning-/ (accessed 5 February 2016).

Newdick, C. (2005) *Who Should We Treat? Rights, Rationing, and Resources in the NHS* (2nd edn). Oxford: Oxford University Press.

NHS Choices (2015) *Scoliosis.* Available at: www.nhs.uk/conditions/scoliosis/pages/ introduction.aspx (accessed 5 February 2016).

Nordahl, C.W., Simon, T.J., Zierhut, C., Solomon, M., Rogers, S.J. and Amaral, D.G. (2008) Brief report: methods for acquiring structural MRI data in very young children with autism without the use of sedation. *Journal of Autism and Development Disorder,* 38: 1581–1590. Available at: http:// ebscohost.com (accessed 16 December 2014).

O'Reilly, R. (2014) Improving the management of patients with autism. *Imaging Therapy and Practice,* 16–21.

Parellada, M., Boada, L., Moreno, C., Llorente, C., Romo, J., Muela, C. et al. (2013) Speciality care programme for autism spectrum disorders in an urban population: a case-management model for health care delivery in an ASD population. *European Psychiatry,* 28: 102–109.

Pfeil, M. and Howe, A. (2004) Ensuring primary care reaches the 'hard to reach'. *Quality in Primary Care,* 12: 185–90.

Positive About Autism™ (2014) *Positive About Autism™.* Available at: http:// positiveaboutautism.co.uk/ (accessed 5 February 2016).

Rhoades, R.A., Scarpa, A. and Salley, B. (2007) The importance of physician knowledge of autism spectrum disorder: results of a parent survey. *BMC Pediatrics,* 37(7). Available at: http://link.springer.com.salford.idm.oclc.org/article/10.1186/1471-2431-7-37/fulltext.html (accessed 26 June 2016).

Romanczyk, R.G., Gillis, J.M., Noyes-Grosser, D.M., Holland, J.P., Holland, C.L. and Lyons, D. (2005) Clinical clues, developmental milestones, and early identification/assessment of children with disabilities; practical applications and conceptual considerations. *Infants and Young Children,* 18(3): 212–221.

Samtani, A., Sterling-Levis, K., Scholten, R., Woolfenden, S., Hooft, L. and Williams, K. (2011) *Diagnostic Tests for Autism Spectrum Disorders (ASD) in Preschool Children (Protocol).* The Cochrane Collaboration.

Scarpinato, N., Bradley, J., Kurbjun, K., Bateman, X., Holtzer, B. and Ely, B. (2010) Caring for the child with an autism spectrum disorder in the acute setting. *Journal for Specialists in Pediatric Nursing,* 15(3): 244–254.

Shieve, L.A., Gonzalez, V., Boulet, S.L., Visser, S.N., Rice, C.E., Braun, K.V. et al. (2012) Concurrent medical conditions and health care use and needs among children with learning and behavioural development disabilities, National Health Interview Survey, 2006a-2010. *Research in Developmental Disabilities,* 33: 467–476.

Singh, S.P., Paul, M., Ford, T., Kramer, T., Weaver, T., McLaren, S. et al. (2010) Process, outcome and experience of transition from child to adult mental healthcare: multiperspective study. *The British Journal of Psychiatry,* 197, 305–312.

Stevens, A. and Gillam, A. (1998). Needs assessment: from theory to practice. *British Medical Journal,* 316: 1448–1452.

Stevenson, C.J., Pharoah, P.O. and Stevenson, R. (1997) Cerebral palsy – the transition from youth to adulthood. *Developmental Medicine and Child Neurology,* 39: 336–342.

The National Autistic Society (2015) *Health Workers: Everything You Need to Know.* Available at: www.autism.org.uk/professionals/health-workers.aspx (accessed 5 February 2016).

_____(2013) *Push for Action; We Need to Turn the Autism Act into Action.* London: The National Autistic Society.

_____(2015) *Social Stories: Their Uses and Benefits.* Available at: http://www.autism.org.uk/about/strategies/social-stories-comic-strips/uses-benefits.aspx (accessed 8 August 2016).

Tregnago, M. and Cheak-Zamora, N.C. (2012) Systematic review of disparities in health care for individuals with autism spectrum disorders in the United States. *Research in Autism Spectrum Disorders,* 6: 1023–1031.

UNICEF (2011) *The State of the World's Children 2011.* New York: United Nations Children's Fund.

United Nations (1989) *The Convention on the Rights of the Child.* New York: United Nations General Assembly.

Van Der Valt, J.H. and Moran, C. (2001) An audit of perioperative management of autistic children. *Paediatric Anaesthesia,* 11(4): 401–408.

Vaz, I. (2013) Visual symbols in healthcare settings for children with learning disabilities and autism spectrum disorder. *British Journal of Nursing,* 22(3): 156–159.

Walsh, N. and Hall, I. (2012) The autism strategy: implications for people with austism and for service development. *Advances in Mental Health and Intellectual Disabilities,* 6(3): 113–120.

Watson, A. R. (2000) Non-compliance and transfer from paediatric to adult transplant unit. *Pediatric Nephrology,* 14: 469–472. Available at: http://search.proquest.com/ (accessed 22 May 2015).

Watson, R., Parr, J.R., Joyce, C., May, C. and Le Couteur, A.S. (2011) Models of transitional care for young people with complex health needs: a scoping review. *Child: Care, Health and Development,* 37(6): 780–791.

Whiteley, P., Todd, L., Carr, K. and Shattock, P. (2010) Gender Ratios in Autism, Asperger Syndrome and Autism Spectrum Disorder. *Autism Insights, 2:* 17–24.

Wilkinson, J.R. and Murray, S.A. (1998) Health needs assessment: assessment in primary care: practical issues and possible approaches. *British Medical Journal,* 316: 1524–1528.

Williams, R. and Wright, J. (1998) Epidemiological issues in health needs assessments. *British Medical Journal,* 316: 1379–1382.

World Health Organization (2015) *Maternal, newborn, child and adolescent health.* Available at: www.who.int/maternal_child_adolescent/topics/adolescence/dev/en/ (accessed 5 February 2016).

Wright, J., Williams, R. and Wilkinson, J.R. (1998) Development and importance of health needs assessment. *British Medical Journal,* 316: 1310–1313.

5

UNDERSTANDING THE SOCIAL EXCLUSION OF ROMA

Lisa Scullion and Philip Brown

Chapter overview: **key messages**

- Roma are recognised as one of the most socially excluded communities across contemporary Europe.
- There are a range of structural and cultural barriers impacting on health outcomes, educational attainment, employment, housing and social welfare.
- Policy and practice has increasingly focused on addressing the exclusion of Roma at a European and national level; however, many initiatives do not offer long-term solutions.
- Future approaches to Roma inclusion need to ensure the involvement of Roma in their development and implementation.

Introduction

Roma are recognised as one of the European Union's (EU) largest minority ethnic groups, with estimates that there are more than 10 million Roma residing across the EU (Council of Europe (CoE), 2011; European Commission (EC), 2012). Despite a commitment at a European level to address the continuing disadvantage of Roma, and the development of a number of policy initiatives, entrenched disadvantage, discrimination, prejudice and exclusion remain defining features in the lives of many Roma (Amnesty International, 2011; CoE, 2011b; EC, 2011). Indeed, it is widely acknowledged that Roma are one of the most socially excluded communities across contemporary Europe (Amnesty International, 2011; Bartlett, Benini, and Gordon, 2011; CoE, 2011b; EC, 2011; ERIO, 2010).

The chapter begins by defining and clarifying our use of the term Roma and the concept of social exclusion. We then outline some of the key characteristics of the exclusion of Roma, with reference to the specific policy areas of housing, health, education and employment. We provide a discussion of the European and UK policy context, before exploring what is currently known about Roma communities who have migrated to the UK. The discussion includes a case study of a mediation project aimed at increasing interactions between Roma and non-Roma communities. Finally, the chapter concludes by highlighting the issues that need considering in order to continue to address the exclusion of Roma.

Defining Roma

The term 'Roma', first chosen at the inaugural World Romani Congress held in London in 1971, is now widely accepted across the European Union (EU) as a generic and pragmatic term to describe a diverse range of communities. Members of these communities can differ in many significant linguistic and cultural ways and include people who identify themselves as Roma, Sinti and Kale, whose ancestors originate from northern India. Similarly, it can also include other indigenous groups in countries across the EU such as Gypsies and Travellers resident in Ireland and the UK, and Yenish communities living in Switzerland and France, who do not routinely see themselves as part of the Roma community (CoE, 2011a). As such, '"the Roma" are a particularly difficult social group to conceptualise accurately' (Kovats, 2001: 7–8) due to the complexities associated with identities which are bound up in culture, time, practices, ethnicity, language, national identifications and so on. Indeed, for some commentators, using a homogenising label of Roma is problematic, particularly when such definitions are used for policy purposes (Matras, 2013).

While we recognise that the term 'Roma' is disputed, and acknowledge that debates around the conceptualisation of Roma are ongoing, for the purpose of this chapter our discussions utilise the Council of Europe (CoE) definition, which uses the term 'Roma' to refer to:

> Roma, Sinti, Kale and related groups in Europe, including Travellers and the Eastern groups (Dom and Lom), and covers the wide diversity of the groups concerned, including persons who identify themselves as Gypsies. (CoE, 2006: 4)

However, within a UK policy and practice framework the use of the term Roma tends to refer to those populations who arrived in the UK from other countries, usually those within Central and Eastern Europe. Here, the term Gypsies, Roma and Travellers (GRT) is commonly used to encompass a diverse group which includes Roma who have migrated to the UK and indigenous Gypsy and Traveller communities (often associated with caravan dwelling). There are broad similarities between UK Gypsy and Traveller populations and Roma communities: a history of nomadism, and issues relating to generally poor health outcomes, educational attainment, and other indicators of social exclusion. However, there are also huge differences between these populations, not least relating to the fact that Roma in the UK are by and large migrants, and as such face similar issues to other newly arriving communities (for example, language barriers, lack of understanding of UK systems, etc.). This chapter focuses specifically on those communities who are identified as 'Roma', and within the UK, this primarily relates to those who have migrated from Central and Eastern European (CEE) countries. In terms of UK Gypsy and Traveller communities; discussions of social exclusion relating to these populations can be found elsewhere (see, for example, Kenrick and Clark, 1999; Clark and Greenfields, 2006; Brown and Scullion, 2010).

Reflection

What issues come to mind when you see or hear the term Roma?

The social exclusion of Roma: a 'European issue'

Social exclusion is a much debated and highly contested concept within social science (see, for example, Room, 1995), but one that has become firmly embedded in the policy discourses of many European countries (Béland, 2007). Originating in France, the term is linked to the concept of citizenship which views:

> [S]ociety as a status hierarchy comprising people bound together by rights and obligations that reflect, and are defined with respect to, a shared moral order. Exclusion is the state of detachment from this moral order and can be brought about by many factors, including limited income. (Walker, 1995: 103)

While poverty is a key constituent of social exclusion, the concept of social exclusion has moved debates beyond an economic focus, to consider the ways in which 'discrimination, chronic ill health, geographical location or cultural identification' (Hills et al., 2002: 6) may constrain individuals from effective participation in society. Indeed, a comprehensive review of disadvantage undertaken by UK academics defines social exclusion as:

> A complex and multi-dimensional process. It involves the lack or denial of resources, rights, goods and services, and the inability to participate in the normal relationships and activities, available to the majority of people in a society, whether in economic, social, cultural or political arenas (Levitas et al., 2007: 9).

People who experience such exclusion 'across more than one domain or dimension of disadvantage' (Levitas et al., 2007: 9) are regarded as suffering deep or severe social exclusion, a situation that many commentators agree is common for Roma communities across contemporary Europe (see, for example, Bartlett, Benini and Gordon, 2011: ERIO, 2010). It is impossible to adequately understand the social exclusion experienced by 'migrant' Roma populations without first appreciating the context within which Roma have lived in their countries of origin. The following provides an overview of some of the issues and barriers Roma face across Europe in relation to four key policy areas: housing, health, education and employment.

Housing

The accommodation of Roma and issues related to the segregation occurring between Roma and non-Roma populations are central to the concerns around social exclusion. Indeed, housing issues are often at the root of a variety of associated negative impacts in the lives of Roma. A review of housing provision in 15 European countries, for example, found clear evidence that Roma were particularly disadvantaged:

> [Roma] suffer from a combination of neglect in terms of housing provision and control in terms of settlement. This is reflected in their housing circumstances, which are typically highly segregated, deprived and excluded from mainstream society. (Phillips, 2010: 218)

Across Central and Eastern Europe a lack of adequate housing remains a pervasive issue for Roma. In Bulgaria and Hungary, for example, many Roma live in segregated 'ghettos' or 'colonies', while in Slovakia 50 per cent of Roma are reported as living in settlements – which lack basic service provision – on the outskirts of towns and villages (Molnár et al., 2011). There are also examples of walls being built between Roma settlements and the majority population to keep the two communities apart (European Roma Rights Centre, ERRC, 2010). In the UK some resentment and hostility towards Roma has been observed following EU expansion. This resentment led to specific consequences in Northern Ireland, for example, where Roma who had recently migrated there were forced out of their homes in 2009 following pressure from the local majority population (McGarry, 2011).

Health

Endemic poverty, poor housing conditions and a lack of basic amenities and sanitation in the locations in which many Roma live contribute to ill health among Roma populations across Europe. Indeed, '[for Roma] life expectancy is in general 8–15 years lower and the mortality, infectious and chronic disease rates are much higher' (CoE, 2011b: 9). Such outcomes have many causes, including poverty, lack of access to health services, poor quality of health services in areas populated by Roma and prejudice of health workers. Similarly, it is important to appreciate the intersection between culture and health. Romani culture encompasses different beliefs about health and medical care, and often differences in treatments and procedures lead to confusion when the Roma seek healthcare and healthcare workers are unfamiliar with their culture (Vivian and Dundes, 2004: 88). In the UK specifically, practitioners in a study in Sheffield highlighted that the following health issues were being found among Roma communities: diabetes, heart disease, obesity, teenage pregnancy, nutritional deficiencies, neonatal issues relating to consanguinity, and Hepatitis A, B and C and TB, with Hepatitis and TB posing difficulties in relation to tracing and screening, particularly if the communities were mobile (Ratcliffe, 2011).

Reflection

What do you understand by the term social exclusion?

In what ways is social exclusion manifested for Roma communities?

Education (and children)

Evidence suggests that Roma children are a particularly disadvantaged group within an already marginalised population (Farkas, 2007). Some of the key – and widely acknowledged – issues facing Roma children include low levels of attendance at schools (particularly in relation to secondary education), and poor educational attainment compared to majority populations (Bartlett, Benini and Gordon, 2011; CoE, 2011a). As a result of 'sporadic and unsystematic school attendance' (Symeou et al., 2009: 514), it is reported that illiteracy rates among Roma are often in excess of 50 per cent (CoE, 2011b). The intersection of education and poverty has been highlighted as a key issue, with day-to-day survival underpinning the lives of many Roma (Scullion and Brown, 2013). As such, children are sometimes expected to contribute to the family income by themselves undertaking paid employment, or by looking after younger siblings so parents can work (Scullion and Brown, 2013). Furthermore, in addition to residential segregation (highlighted above), it has emerged that educational segregation is 'systemic' in some European countries (see ERRC, 2004, 2011; Friedman et al., 2009; O'Nions, 2010; Ryder, Rostas and Taba, 2014). The ERRC (2004), for example, talks about three different types of segregation in relation to Roma: segregation in 'special' schools for children with developmental disabilities (often through direct placement, i.e. without prior enrolment in mainstream schools), segregation within mainstream schools and segregation in 'ghetto schools'. Additionally, Roma children are significantly overrepresented in public care systems in many European countries.

Reflection

The separation of Roma children into different schools or classes remains a practice in certain places across Europe. Why do you think such an approach persists?

Employment

Paid employment levels for Roma vary across Europe but are routinely significantly lower than those of majority populations. A high level of discrimination against Roma jobseekers is also apparent in many settings (Bartlett, Benini and Gordon, 2011; EC, 2011a). Recent research has characterised Roma employment in terms of horizontal and vertical segregation in the labour market, with segregation into low skilled, low paid and precarious/unstable employment, coupled with limited opportunities to progress (Scullion, Brown and Dwyer, 2014). Gender is also a feature of discussions around economic activity, with reports of higher levels of unemployment among Roma women, particularly young women (Pantea, 2014) and the view that gender barriers were more pronounced within the Roma community (Lajčáková, 2014). Furthermore, it has been acknowledged that increasing secondary education among Roma does not increase employment rates in the same way that it would for non-Roma (ibid). Across, access to many unemployment benefits has become increasingly dependent on recipients accepting compulsory work or training opportunities (see Lødemel and Trickey, 2001). In some countries – for example, Hungary and Slovakia – such work programmes are primarily undertaken by Roma. Some Roma have made use of their rights to free movement to escape endemic prejudice in their countries of origin and seek work in other European nations – including the UK (Scullion and Pemberton, 2010).

Reflection

To what extent is the culture of Roma populations responsible for the social exclusion they face?

To what extent are structural factors responsible?

In recognition of the pervasive and ongoing disadvantage and marginalisation of Roma highlighted above, the institutions of the European Union are openly involved – and have been for many years – in a number of initiatives to improve the lives of Roma (Bartlett, Benini and Gordon, 2011; McGarry, 2011), with what some call a 'Europeanization of Roma policy' (Vermeersch, 2011: 96). In 2008, a Commission Staff Working Document (CSWD) set in motion a series of steps that would lead to the development of what was perceived as a framework for a more effective implementation of policies to support Roma inclusion within each Member State of the EU (Commission of the European Communities, 2008). Consequently, in 2011, the European Commission published the *EU Framework for National Roma Integration Strategies up to 2020,* which called on all European Union Member States to prepare, or adapt, strategic documents to meet four key EU Roma integration goals: access to education, employment, healthcare and housing (referred to as National Roma Integration Strategies or NRIS), including 'targeted actions and sufficient funding (national, EU and other) to deliver' on the goals (European Commission, 2011: 4).

By March 2012, all European Union Member States had presented their NRIS, or a set of policy measures, in light of this EU Framework. These strategies varied depending on the size of the Roma population and the challenges that countries felt that they needed to address (European Commission, 2012). The NRIS were expected to be linked to overall social inclusion policies within individual countries to ensure *mainstreaming* of Roma inclusion rather than *separation.* Furthermore, it was stated that regional and local authorities had a key role to play, as they would be responsible for the implementation of integration strategies on the ground. Effective monitoring of performance against these strategies was encouraged as was the integral role of Roma civic society, and regional and local authorities in their design, implementation and evaluation.

However, it is recognised that progress has been slow (European Commission, 2014) with initiatives not always delivering intended outcomes or providing only short-term solutions (Brown et al., 2014; 2015). Approaches across European countries vary, but broadly speaking they fall into two camps: *targeted schemes* (i.e. focusing specifically on Roma) or more *mainstream approaches,* with a broader focus (i.e. unemployed people, minority ethnic communities, etc.). What is clear is that, regardless of the approach, there is often a disconnect between the strategies that are put in place and their actual impact on the ground. The main reasons cited for the limited effectiveness of existing mechanisms are lack of political will, lack of strong partnerships and coordination mechanisms, but also an unwillingness to acknowledge the needs of Roma as an issue (European Commission, 2010). Furthermore, there are particular concerns around a lack of involvement of Roma in the consultation, development and implementation of initiatives (Brown et al., 2015).

Arguably, part of the challenge also relates to competing discourses around Roma exclusion. More specifically, Roma typically primarily emphasise *structural factors* such as poverty, discrimination and racism and describe the negative impact that these issues have on their daily lives (Brown, Dwyer and Scullion, 2013: 54). On the other hand non Roma (including some of those responsible for the development and implementation of policy and various services) often view the social exclusion of Roma as 'being rooted in the dysfunctional behaviour or culture of Roma themselves' (Brown, Dwyer and Scullion, 2013: 54). Indeed, racisms (see Husband, 1987), that use individual, physical and/or collective cultural differences between communities to legitimise discriminatory practices are important issues that need to be considered in relation to the ongoing exclusion of Roma.

Reflection
_____

How might competing discourses on the social exclusion of Roma impact on the policies and initiatives that are developed?

Roma in the UK

Roma migration to the UK has a long-standing history and has been a continuing feature making up the tapestry of migration flows since 1945 (Horton and Grayson, 2008). However, since 1989, the number of Roma migrating from Central and Eastern Europe (CEE) has steadily increased (Poole, 2010). During the 1990s and early 2000, a number of Roma came to the UK seeking asylum. However, the accession of a number of CEE migrants into the EU led to freedom of movement within EU borders to Roma communities (Poole, 2010). Consequently, those who were once 'forced' migrants were deemed 'voluntary' migrants. Some commentators suggest, however, that Roma still fall into a 'grey area' between 'forced' and voluntary' migration:

> [G]iven the ongoing infringements of Roma rights in CEE, it is not unreasonable to view the Roma as a group that continue to be 'pushed' abroad as much as being 'pulled'. (Poole, 2010: 251)

Although there are widely acknowledged difficulties in enumerating Roma populations (Clark, 1998), research suggested that as of 2013 there were around 200,000 Roma living across the UK (Brown, Martin and Scullion, 2013, 2014). The most numerous nationalities of Roma in the UK are suggested to be Czech, Slovak and Romanian Roma, with the largest populations in cities across the

North of England, East Midlands, Kent, north and east London (European Dialogue, 2009: 38), with groupings in Glasgow (Scotland), Cardiff (Wales) and Belfast (Northern Ireland) (Craig, 2011). Settlement patterns often reflect areas where Roma have been asylum seekers in the past, or where they have existing contacts (European Dialogue, 2009).

A survey carried out by European Dialogue (2009) with Roma living in different areas of England highlighted that Roma have been moving to England because they experience relatively low levels of discrimination here. Indeed, some respondents said they felt proud of their identity for the first time in their lives (European Dialogue, 2009: 7). This survey (involving 104 Roma across ten different locations) found that work was a key motivation for migration, with 58.7 per cent indicating they had moved to England due to greater employment opportunities. Following employment, the main reasons cited were 'a better life for children' (22.1 per cent) and 'discrimination in country of origin' (15.4 per cent). The majority of those surveyed (97.1 per cent) said that their life had improved since coming to England; however, the report raises the question as to whether or not Roma have low expectations due to their experiences in their home countries (see European Dialogue, 2009: 7–8).

Issues for policy and practice

Within the UK, policy makers and practitioners have often conflated the issue of Roma in the UK with discussions around UK Gypsy and Traveller population. At a central government level, there has been limited commitment to producing a specific National Roma Integration Strategy (NRIS) in line with the majority other European countries. Instead, a series of steps taken by government around greater inclusion towards Gypsy and Traveller populations only focussed on Roma arriving from overseas when these issues overlapped with education (Department for Communities and Local Government, 2012).

Given this 'policy vacuum', it is argued that local agencies have had to adopt their own approaches to Roma inclusion, often largely driven by their current approach to other minority ethnic communities (including UK Gypsies and Travellers) (Craig, 2011: 23). As highlighted previously, while it is recognised that there are similarities between indigenous Gypsy and Traveller populations and migrant Roma communities, there are also considerable differences relating to language barriers, lack of understanding of UK systems, and the degree to which Roma have experienced extreme financial hardship, discrimination and exclusion in their home countries. Indeed, recognising the wider home country experiences of Roma is vital to understanding their engagement with service areas in the UK. Such issues are sometimes compounded by the concentration of Roma in particular geographical areas, with very little contact with members of the wider community. Research carried out in Manchester, for example, highlighted that Roma often choose to live in close proximity to extended family, with little desire or need to form friendships outside their own communities; however, this was sometimes – although not always – attributed to a desire to avoid conflict (Davies and Murphy, 2010). As such, from a practice perspective, there are particular considerations around engaging with Roma communities, with suggestions by some frontline services that Roma communities require an increased level of support in comparison to other minority ethnic and migrant groups (Scullion and Brown, 2013).

Approaches based on mediation techniques as a means of reducing inequalities and 'bridging' the gap between communities has been a significant focus not just within the UK, but also across Europe (Brown et al., 2014). This approach ranges from the training of Roma community members to provide a link between communities and services, through to 'trusted' frontline staff undertaking an intensive role within Roma communities. Such approaches have often – but not exclusively – focused on addressing inequalities in relation to health and children's education. However, beyond these specific policy areas, mediation has also gained momentum as a means of fostering cross-community relations at a local level to promote greater inter-cultural understanding (ibid). The case study below provides an example of how football has been used as a mediation technique to improve relations between Roma and non-Roma young people in Bradford.

Case study: **Football as a tool for cross-community mediation**

Migration Yorkshire commissioned the Joshua Project, a Bradford-based voluntary organisation working with socially excluded children and young people from a range of backgrounds, to run a cross-community mediation project with a particular focus on young members of the Roma community. The Joshua Project noticed a lack of cohesion between Roma and non-Roma young people and often had to intervene to halt potential confrontations and racist verbal abuse from non-Roma. The Joshua Project had observed through their community work that one activity that brought different cultures together was football. They had an existing football team and wanted to open this up to Roma young people. The aim was to use football as a tool to promote cohesion, as well as giving Roma young people the opportunity to engage in a free, healthy, positive activity.

The Joshua Project held an open training session as part of a community festival in a local park. Over 30 Roma young people attended, in addition to existing team members. Rather than continuing to train on existing football pitches they ran the club from the local park each week. The activity was supported by a football coach and three youth workers. The football coach provided the technical training while the youth workers informally used existing Show Racism the Red Card (SRTRC) resources to encourage the young people to recognise similarities but to also see the value of celebrating difference.

◆

The project was successful in its aim to encourage cohesion and a greater understanding on the football field, but this also spread to 'street football' as well as other areas of community life, with the team mentality bringing the young people together. For example, the Joshua Project observed Roma and non-Roma young people meeting outside of football training to play football together as well as more mixing of the young people at the open youth club. The Joshua Project is now transferring some of the techniques applied to the football club to other youth activities and clubs to encourage more demographically representative participation.

While there are many examples of positive initiatives, we need to recognise the changing social, economic and political context in which 'Roma inclusion' is situated. First, the expansion of the EU to include Bulgaria and Romania, countries that are home to large Roma populations. There has also been a gradual change in the framing of the discourse about the place of the UK within the EU and the often largely negative discussions around EU migration, with concerns raised around the perceived impacts on housing, welfare and employment. For the most part, the deeply rooted discrimination experienced by so many Roma has not yet transferred into everyday discourse within the UK. However, there are signs that this is unfortunately beginning to change with an increase in negative media around Roma communities in particular geographical areas, for example the intervention in the media by the former Home Secretary David Blunkett in November 2013 (see BBC News, 2013).

At the same time, efforts to address the exclusion of Roma are taking place within a constrained economic context and the very services that often work with Roma communities in the UK (for example, the local authority Traveller Education Support Service or Ethnic Minority and Traveller Attainment Services) are the ones that have often seen their services eroded by cutbacks given the lack of ring-fenced funding (Bartlett et al., 2011: 103). The combination of a reduction in funding for areas that would support greater integration and mitigate some of the inequalities and a seemingly growing hostility to migrants in the UK raises significant concerns for Roma inclusion within the UK in the future.

Reflection

What are some of the issues faced by professionals working with Roma communities?

How could services be better designed to accommodate the range of issues faced by Roma communities?

Conclusion

This chapter has focused on outlining the social exclusion of Roma populations who have migrated to the UK in recent years. This is set against a European policy context which, in recent years, has increasingly focused on trying to systematically tackle some of the core elements of social exclusion in education, employment, health and housing. The experience of such populations in their 'home' countries is particularly important, and this shows that Roma have invariably experienced poor outcomes across a range of service areas, discrimination, under-representation in the democratic process and high levels of poverty in the majority of countries in which they feature. For those who can afford to leave their country of origin, their migration to the UK is then a combination of these 'push' factors as well as the opportunity the UK often presents for improving their life chances. However, exclusion experienced by Roma often persists into the UK. This may be exacerbated by the reductions to funding for agencies experienced and equipped to work with minority populations, as well as a broader anti-migrant discourse.

While we need to acknowledge and understand the exclusion faced by Roma communities, it is also essential to note that there are a number of areas where Roma and non-Roma populations live relatively harmoniously as one part of an often very diverse community. A large number of Roma households are working in a variety of industries, skilled and unskilled, and Roma children are typically enrolled in local schools. Furthermore, as highlighted in research with Roma (see European Dialogue, 2009; Brown et al., 2013), discussions with Roma have suggested that their migration and settlement within the UK – and other Member States – has been a way to escape the constructed limitations and exclusions of being solely defined by their ethnicity as Roma.

Recommended reading

- Goodwin, K. and De Hert, P. (2013) *European Roma Integration Efforts – A Snapshot*, Brussels: Brussels University Press.

- Ryder, A., Cemlyn, S. and Acton, T.A. (2014). *Hearing the Voices of Gypsy, Roma and Traveller Communities: Inclusive Community Development*. Bristol: Policy Press.

- Sigona, N. and Trehan, N. (eds) (2009) *Romani Politics in Europe: Poverty, Ethnic Marginalisation and the Neoliberal Order.* Basingstoke: Palgrave.

Relevant web links

- www.romasource.eu
- www.romamatrix.eu
- www.errc.org/resource-centre
- www.erionet.eu/
- www.coe.int/en/web/portal/roma

References

Amnesty International (2011) *Briefing: Human Rights on the Margins, Roma in Europe,* London: Amnesty International.

Bartlett, W., Benini, R. and Gordon, C. (2011) *Measures to Promote the Situation of Roma Citizens in the European Union,* Report for the European Parliament. Brussels: Directorate-General for Internal Policies, Policy Department C Citizens' Rights and Constitutional Affairs.

Béland, D. (2007) The social exclusion discourse: ideas and policy change. *Policy & Politics,* 35(1): 123–139.

Brown, P., Dwyer, P., Martin, P. and Scullion, L. (2014) *Roma Matrix Interim Research Report,* Salford: University of Salford. Available at: https://romamatrix.eu/roma-matrix-interim-research-report (accessed 6 February 2016).

Brown, P., Dwyer, P., Martin, P., Scullion, L. and Turley, H. (2015) *Rights, Responsibilities and Redress? Research on Policy and Practice for Roma Inclusion in Ten Member States.* Salford: University of Salford. Available at: https://romamatrix.eu/research/final-research-report (accessed 7 February 2016).

Brown, P., Dwyer, P. and Scullion, L. (2012) *Roma SOURCE: Interim Report,* report for Roma SOURCE (Sharing of Understanding Rights and Citizenship in Europe) project. Salford: University of Salford. Available at: www.romasource.eu/resources/research/ (accessed 7 February 2016).

_____(2013) *The Limits of Inclusion? Exploring the Views of Roma and Non-Roma in Six European Union Member States,* report for Roma SOURCE (Sharing of Understanding Rights and Citizenship in Europe) project. Salford: University of Salford. Available at: www.romasource.eu/resources/research/ (accessed 7 February 2016).

Brown, P., Martin, P. and Scullion, L. (2013) *Migrant Roma in the United Kingdom: Population Size and Experiences of Local Authorities and Partners.* Salford: The University of Salford.

_____(2014) Migrant Roma in the United Kingdom and the need to estimate population size. *People, Place and Policy,* 8(1): 19–33.

Brown, P. and Scullion, L. (2010) Doing research with Gypsy-Travellers in England: Reflections on experience and practice. *Community Development Journal,* 45: 169–185.

Clark, C. (1998) Counting backwards: the Roma 'numbers game' in Central and Eastern Europe. *Radical Statistics,* 68: 4.

Clark, C. and Greenfields, M. (2006) *Here to Stay: The Gypsies and Travellers of Britain.* Hatfield: University of Hertfordshire Press.

Commission of the European Communities (2008) *Commission Staff Working Document. Accompanying the Communication from the Commission to the European Parliament, the Council, the European Economic and Social Committee and the Committee of the Regions. Non-Discrimination and Equal Opportunities: A Renewed Commitment Community Instruments and Policies for Roma Inclusion.* Brussels: European Commission.

CoE (2006) *Roma and Travellers Glossary.* Brussels: Council of Europe.

_____(2011a) *Defending Roma Human Rights in Europe.* Brussels: Council of Europe.

_____(2011b) *Protecting the Rights of Roma.* Strasbourg: Council of Europe.

Craig, G. (2011) *United Kingdom: Promoting Social Inclusion of Roma: A Study of National Policies,* European Commission. Available at: http://ec.europa.eu/social/main. jsp?catId=1025&langId=en&newsId=1407&moreDocuments=yes&tableName=news (accessed 7 February 2016).

Davies, J. and Murphy, J. (2010) *What's Working: Conversations with Manchester's Romanian Roma Community Living in Longsight and Levenshulme,* Manchester City Council Children's Services International New Arrivals, Travellers and Supplementary Schools Team. Available at: www.natt.org.uk/sites/default/files/documents/whats-working.pdf (accessed 7 February 2016).

Department for Communities and Local Government (2012) *Progress Report by the Ministerial Working Group on Tackling Inequalities Experienced by Gypsies and Travellers.* London: DCLG.

European Commission (2011) *Working Together for Roma Inclusion – The EU Framework Explained.* Belgium: European Commission.

_____(2012) *National Roma Integration Strategies: A First Step in the Implementation of the EU Framework.* Belgium: European Commission.

_____(2014) *Report on the Implementation of the EU Framework for National Roma Integration Strategies.* Belgium: European Commission.

European Dialogue (2009) *The Movement of Roma from New EU Member States: A Mapping Survey of A2 and A8 Roma in England, a report prepared for the Department of Children, Schools and Families.* London: European Dialogue.

European Roma Information Office (ERIO) (2010) *Fact Sheet: Breaking the Poverty Cycle of Roma,* Brussels, European Roma Information Office. Available at: http://cloud2.snappages. com/ecc3fa83da15cf423fe3aaa342f545fa355b24f3/Fact%20sheet_Breaking%20 the%20poverty%20circle%20of%20Roma_2010.pdf (accessed 7 February 2016).

European Roma Rights Centre (ERRC) (2004) *Stigmata: Segregated Schooling of Roma in Central and Eastern Europe,* Budapest: European Roma Rights Centre.

_____(2010) *Standards Do Not Apply: Inadequate Housing in Romani Communities.* Budapest: European Roma Rights Centre.

_____(2011) *Factsheet: Roma Rights Record.* Budapest: European Roma Rights Centre.

Farkas, L. (2007) *Segregation of Roma Children in Education: Addressing Structural Discrimination through the Race Equality Directive.* Luxembourg: European Commission.

Friedman, E., Gallová Kriglerová, E., Kubánová, M. and Slosiarik, M. (2009) *School as Ghetto: Systemic Overrepresentation of Roma in Special Education in Slovakia.* Budapest: Roma Education Fund.

Hills, J., Le Grand, J. and Piachaud. D. (eds) (2002) *Understanding Social Exclusion.* Oxford: Oxford University Press.

Horton, M. and Grayson, J. (2008) *Roma New Migrants: Local Research in the UK and European Contexts*, A Conference Report of Roma New Migrants: A Research and Information Day.

Husband, C. (ed.) (1987) *'Race' in Britain: Continuity and Change* (2nd edn). London: Hutchinson.

Kenrick, D. and Clark, C. (1999) *Moving On: The Gypsies and Travellers of Britain*. Hatfield: University of Hertfordshire Press.

Kovats, M. (2001) Problems of Intellectual and Political Accountability in Respect of Emerging European Roma Policy. *Journal on Ethnopolitics and Minority Issues in Europe (JEMIE)*, 1/2001: 1–10.

Lajčáková J. (2014) Roma MATRIX Country Report: Slovakia. Available at: https:// romamatrix.eu/slovakia-country-report (accessed 7 February 2016).

Levitas, R., Pantazis, C., Fahmy, E., Gordon, D., Lloyd, E. and Patsios, D. (2007) *The Multi-Dimensional Analysis of Social Exclusion*, Report for the Social Exclusion Task Force. London: The Cabinet Office.

Lødemel and Trickey (2001) *An Offer You Can't Refuse: Workfare in International Perspective*. Bristol: The Policy Press.

Matras, Y. (2013) *Scholarship and the Politics of Romani Identity: Strategic and Conceptual Issues*, RomIdent Working Papers No. 1, University of Manchester. Available at: http:// romani.humanities.manchester.ac.uk/virtuallibrary/librarydb/web/files/pdfs/354/ Paper1.pdf (accessed 7 February 2016).

McGarry, A. (2011) The Roma voice in the European Union: between national belonging and transnational identity. *Social Movement Studies*, 10(3): 283–297.

Molnár, Á., Ádám, B., Antova, T., Bosak, L. ,Dimitrov, P., Mileva, H., Pekarcikova, J., Zurlyte, I., Gulis, G., Ádány, R. and Kósa, K. (2011) Health impact assessment of Roma housing policies in Central and Eastern Europe: a comparative analysis. *Environmental Impact Assessment Review*, 32(1): 7–14.

O'Nions, H. (2010) Different and unequal: the educational segregation of Roma pupils in Europe, *Intercultural Education*, 21(1): 1–13.

Pantea, M.C. (2014) Roma MATRIX Country Report: Romania. Available at: https:// romamatrix.eu/romania-country-report (accessed 7 February 2016).

Poole, L. (2010) National action plans for social inclusion and A8 migrants: the case of the Roma in Scotland. *Critical Social Policy*, 30: 245–266.

Phillips, D. (2010) Minority ethic segregation, integration and citizenship: a European perspective. *Journal of Ethnic and Minority Studies*, 36(2): 209–225.

Ratcliffe, G. (2011) *The needs of the Slovak Roma community in Sheffield: A summary report*. Sheffield: NHS Sheffield.

Room, G. (ed.) (1995) *Beyond the threshold: the measurement and analysis of social exclusion*. Bristol: The Policy Press.

Ryder, A.R., Rostas, I. and Taba, M. (2014) 'Nothing about us without us': the role of inclusive community development in school desegregation for Roma communities. *Race Ethnicity and Education*, 17(4): 518–539.

Scullion, L. and Brown, P. (2013) *'What's working?': Promoting the Inclusion of Roma in and through Education: Transnational policy review and research report*. Salford: University of Salford.

Scullion, Brown and Dwyer (2014) *'You cannot consider it a job because it just gives us food for a day': Roma, paid work and unemployment*, Paper presented to the Social Policy

Association Symposium on Roma Integration in the European Union, the University of Sheffield, 15 July 2014.

Scullion, L. and Pemberton, S. (2010) *Exploring Migrant Workers Motivations for Migration and Their Perceived Contributions to the UK: A Case Study of Liverpool.* Salford: The University of Salford.

Symeou, L., Karagiorgi, Y., Roussounidou, E. and Kaloyirou, C. (2009) Roma and their education in Cyprus: reflections on INSETRom teacher training for Roma inclusion. *Intercultural Education*, 20(6): 511–521.

Vermeersch, P. (2011) Roma and mobility in the European Union. In K. Pietarinen (ed.) *Roma and Traveller Inclusion in Europe. Green Questions and Answers.* Belgium: Green European Foundation: 91–97.

Vivian, C. and Dundes, L. (2004) The crossroads of culture and health among the Roma (Gypsies). *Journal of Nursing Scholarship*, 36(1): 86–91.

Walker, R. (1995) The dynamics of poverty and social exclusion, pp.102–128 in G. Room (ed.) *Beyond the Threshold: The Measurement and Analysis of Social Exclusion.*

6

TRANS AND GENDER DIVERSITY: MESSAGES FOR POLICY AND PRACTICE

Michaela Rogers

Chapter overview: **key messages**

- As trans people increasingly gain visibility in social life, so too do the social problems that affect them.
- Theoretical concepts such as heteronormativity, gender normativity and cisgenderism help to facilitate an understanding of trans people's social exclusion and marginalisation.
- Key policies offer recognition and legal protection for some trans people, but this is limited to those who identify within the confines of the gender binary.
- There are multiple barriers for trans people accessing health and social care services.

Introduction

Trans is an emerging area of academic interest, and trans people are increasingly visible within our communities, but the social context of trans people's lives is under-explored in academic literature (Rogers, 2013). Notwithstanding, there is a growing body of work which is gaining recognition for its interrogation of gendered life through the lens of trans subjectivity (Hines, 2007; Davy, 2011; Rogers, 2013, 2015). Some of the issues raised within this body of work demonstrate how structural factors (for example, political ideology, legal institutions) impact upon everyday experience (concerning, for example, intimate and familial relationships) and these structural issues will be drawn upon to illustrate the complex nature of trans people's lives.

This chapter focuses on the increasing recognition of trans people along with some of the social problems that affect them. Two of the enduring issues which affects trans communities are those of marginalisation and discrimination (Mitchell and Howarth, 2009; TGEU, 2015a). While the problem of marginalisation is one that is entrenched, over the years there have been advances in policy and legislation intended to increase trans people's equality and rights. Several critiques have been made however, which point to the limitations of policy changes. Moreover, the implementation of these policies has not necessarily increased access to services or participation rates for trans people and the barriers are manifold (Rogers, 2013). An understanding of the operation of heteronormativity, gender normativity and cisgenderism underpins the analysis below, which also explores the nature of these barriers in particular and trans people's social exclusion more generally.

The first part of the chapter will deconstruct key terminology and clarify definitions of trans identity and practice in order to promote an understanding of gender diversity. This discussion will progress to explore heteronormativity, gender normativity and cisgenderism as critical concepts which impact on trans subjectivity. Thus, the first section of the chapter will challenge normative and dominant thinking in relation to gender as a fixed, binary position and as a social characteristic. This will also be achieved by presenting a discussion of trans people's marginalisation and citizenship before critiquing related legislation and policy (including the Gender Recognition Act 2004 and the Equality Act 2010). An analysis of these two pieces of legislation will explore the extent to which trans people's citizenship rights and equality have been enhanced. This discussion will expose some of the barriers that remain, as both Acts are underpinned by and maintain notions of gender as a dichotomous, immutable category. The chapter will end with an exploration of the interface between policy and practice and consider some barriers, challenges and recommendations.

Theoretical and conceptual frameworks

Over the decades the growth of feminist and queer literature has resulted in a sustained and active theorising of the language that we use in relation to sex, gender and sexuality. This discussion is ever-evolving and potentially confusing. Indeed, sex, gender and sexuality are complex areas of inquiry and some have argued that there is a need to separate these debates, particularly as sexuality has been neglected or positioned as secondary to gender (Sedgwick, 1990). A good place to start then, is by defining these key terms in addition to other concepts which are central to an analysis of trans inequality and marginalisation.

Sex, gender and sexuality

The terms 'sex' and 'gender' can be differentiated as 'sex' refers to the physical characteristics of a body assigned as male or female, while 'gender' relates to a social identity which is then associated with a body which is perceived to be sexed in a particular way (Enke, 2012). As such, sex and gender are interconnected. Moreover, in this conceptualisation, sex has an essentialist quality whereas gender can be said to be socially constructed. Accordingly, the idea of gender as binary (a two-part category of male/female) is contingent upon the social conditions within which it is understood. In other words, the process and act of ascribing gender is subject to different contexts in terms of socio-cultural circumstance, time and place. Some authors consider sex to be a social construct too (Butler, 1990, 2004; Fausto-Sterling, 2000). Butler et al. argue that sex is a complex mixture of things, rather than simply a case of identifying genitalia as male or female. Rather, a person's sex is a combination of external genitalia, secondary sex characteristics (for example, breasts, body hair), reproductive and internal sex organs (for example, ovaries and a uterus), chromosomes, hormones (oestrogen, testosterone), psychology, social aspects and more (O'Keefe, 1999; Serano, 2013).

Reflection

Intersex people have male and female, or ambiguous, sex characteristics. Consider an intersex child who is ascribed a male or female identity at birth by a doctor who inspects the baby's genitalia. Try to imagine how it must feel to be a child who has been assigned a male identity and brought up as boy, but who has an intersex condition which means that they also have female physical characteristics (ovaries and a uterus along with the ability to produce the female hormone oestrogen). As they reach puberty their body may start to show the secondary characteristics associated with females as breasts develop.

The dominant Western paradigm of 'sexuality' is also linked to sexed bodies, as assumptions are made about sexuality based upon male and female identity, leading to a theoretical framework which includes opposite-sex attraction (heterosexuality) or same-sex attraction (homosexuality) or attraction to people regardless of sex/gender (bisexuality/pan sexuality). However, Enke (2012) points to the complexity of sexuality as she notes how it refers to a number of aspects such as a person's sexual orientation, expressions, interests, acts and/or experiences. In addition, there are other categories of sexuality including trans sexuality (the sexuality of trans people), asexuality (where people do not identify as sexual beings) and other more marginal categories (see Stryker and Aizura, 2013).

While it is useful to distinguish between sex, gender and sexuality, Serano (2013: 9) argues that it is important to acknowledge that a clear dividing line cannot be drawn 'where each of these categories ends and another begins'. For example, aspects of physical sex (such as genitalia) play a key role in acts of sexuality.

Trans and cisgender

Throughout this chapter I use the term 'trans' as an umbrella term to describe a range of identities and practices including trans, transgender, transsexual, MtF, FtM, androgyne, genderqueer, queer and crossdresser. This list is indicative, not exhaustive. It is hard to capture the heterogeneity of trans identities, but the list given does underline the argument for recognising a *gender spectrum*, rather than a *gender binary*. For many trans people identifying with fixed labels is challenging, as Iantaffi and Bockting (2011) found when conducting a survey with trans communities. Iantaffi and Bockting offered survey respondents a comparatively broad range of gender identity labels to select (for example, trans man, transsexual woman, genderqueer and so on). Yet 29.5 per cent of 1229 respondents chose 'Other'. Clearly, not all people identify within the predetermined binary of male/female, nor do they experience a fixed sense of gender identity. Indeed people who identify as trans, whose gender and/or sex is fluid, or who are 'Other' to male and female, disrupt the assumption that sex/gender fall into binary categories (Monro, 2007). This troubles some of the early feminist work on patriarchy and gender inequality (see also Butler 1990, 2004; Fausto-Sterling 2000). Furthermore, the growing body of literature on trans has helped a new binary opposition to emerge: cisgender (or cis) and trans. 'Cisgender' derives from the Latin prefix 'cis' meaning on the same side or remaining with the same orientation. The neologism 'cisgender' helps to delineate 'non-trans' people (those whose gender matches that which was ascribed at birth) (Enke, 2012).

Wilchins (2004: 26) offers a concise definition of trans which is contextualised through permanent and temporary embodied practices, as trans identity refers to 'people who cross sexes by changing their bodies (transsexual) and those who cross genders by changing their clothing, behaviour and appearance'. For transsexuals, the distinction between gender (a social and psychological construct) and sex (a biological category) is significant, as transsexual people often explain their feelings of gender dissonance as being born into the 'the wrong body'; this draws attention to the psychological self (gender identity) as separate to and discordant with the physical, sexed body (Prosser 1998; Serano 2007). In law, a transsexual person is someone who 'proposes to undergo, is undergoing or has undergone gender reassignment' (Equality Act 2010) and to access medical intervention. Most transsexuals will be recognised as having gender dysphoria; this is discomfort or distress which is caused by a mismatch between biological sex and gender identity. As suggested by Wilchins, then, transsexual identity sits within the dominant framework for understanding gender, in congruence with the male/female distinction, and can incorporate the desire to permanently reassign the sexed body from male-to-female, or vice versa.

Heteronormativity, cisgenderism and transphobia

The discussion above draws attention to a variety of discourses and in particular one that is underpinned by a belief about gender as binary and heterosexuality as 'normal'; this position is heteronormative. As a conceptualisation, heteronormativity promulgates the belief that gender is either male or female, with the usual trajectory for gendered beings to pursue opposite-sex marriage, to be monogamous and to have children (Warner, 1991). This is the dominant and normative narrative which influences gendered practice in the Western world. Therefore, heteronormativity creates an embedded socio-cultural expectation for individuals to identify with a certain gender (male/female), to be heterosexual and to procreate. This type of thinking has led to the creation of the 'Other', the person who does not identify as male/female, is not heterosexual and who does not live in a family which is configured in a traditionally gendered way.

Yet, in some respects we are living at a time of significant social change where the notion of heteronormativity is being challenged. Indeed, the greater level of social acceptance and visibility of trans people problematises dominant and traditional ideas about gender. Unfortunately, despite the recent emergence of trans as an academic interest, and the ever increasing gaze upon trans in the media and popular culture (Hines, 2013), trans people continue to experience discrimination and there are many aspects of their lives that remain unexplored (Whittle et al., 2007; Hines, 2013). It may be that transphobia (the hatred or fear of trans people) underpins the majority of micro-level (individual) experiences and marginalisation within communities, but structural oppression is not so easily explained by transphobia. Some authors argue that structural oppression is better understood in terms of 'cisgenderism' (Ansara and Hegarty, 2011; Kennedy, 2013). Ansara and Hegarty (2011) define cisgenderism as follows:

> First, unlike 'transphobia', cisgenderism describes a prejudicial *ideology*, rather than an individual *attitude*, that is systemic, multi-level and reflected in authoritative cultural discourses. Second, [...] cisgenderism problematises the categorical distinction itself between classes of people as either 'transgender' or 'cisgender'. (Ansara and Hegarty, 2011: 4, original emphasis)

Unlike transphobia, cisgenderism describes a discriminatory and harmful ideology, rather than an individual attitude, that is systemic, multi-level and deeply engrained in socio-cultural discourses and social institutions. Ansara and Hegarty (2011) propose that cisgenderism should be understood along the same lines of racism or sexism, as an ideology that is divisive and which discriminates. Cisgenderism 'involves multiple intersecting assumptions that construct people's own designations of their genders as less valid ... [and] constructs the world as having only two valid genders and sexes' (Blumer, Ansara and Watson, 2013: 269).

Reflection

Do you agree with the concept of cisgenderism?

Think about how gender is represented, or reflected, in legislation, art, media, literature, religion and others. Reflect on discourses of gender which offer written, spoken or pictorial messages or ideas about gender. Do these messages, or ideas, reflect the belief that gender is a binary concept, or a spectrum?

A marginalised population?

The societal processes and structures through which inequality is ingrained can be understood in terms of invisibility and social exclusion. Monro (2005: 43) describes social exclusion as 'the way in which certain groups lack the resources to participate in wider society and face barriers to participation at institutional and cultural levels'. Several authors argue that the social exclusion of trans people is embedded in social structures as forms of trans discrimination range from media ridicule to hate crime (Gamson, 1998; Valentine 2003; Chakraborti and Hardy, 2015). Despite this, public tolerance is seen to be on the increase. This is evidenced by the growth in popularity of the localised 'Pride' events, a vibrant visibility in the cyber-world and recent successful television airings (for example, 'My Transsexual Summer', a Channel 4 broadcast in 2012, and Louis Theroux's documentary 'Transgender Kids' on BBC1 in 2015). Other authors highlight the limitations of this type of visibility arguing that cisgenderism and transphobia are pervasive, as trans people face disadvantage in many other areas of social life, including employment, access to public services, economic status and in criminal justice systems (Monro, 2005; Whittle et al., 2007; Mitchell and Howarth, 2009; Hines, 2013).

In everyday life, an additional pressure for trans people who publicly seek to perform a male or female identity is the ability to 'pass'. Garfinkel (1967: 118) described the ability to pass as '... the work of achieving and making secure [the] rights to live in the elected sex (gender) status while providing for the possibility of detection and ruin carried out within the socially structured conditions within which this work occurred'. As such, passing is conceived as a strategy which can enable a trans individual to live in their acquired gender free from marginalisation or stigma. In research on trans people's lives the experiences of shame and stigma have been reported to be experienced by respondents and their family members and resulted in the estrangement of trans individuals from their family of origin (Rogers, 2013, 2016). It is clear that the concept of stigma interlocks with the experience of social exclusion. Passing can provide individuals with the potential to negate any potential stigma attracted by identifying as trans and may assist people in their desire for social inclusion, but at the same time, this supports and sustains the dominance of heteronormative aesthetics of male and female (Aoki, 2012). It also reinforces the notion of a gender binary and supports an essentialist paradigm of sex and gender as immutable and natural.

Furthermore, despite the growth of media coverage and increased visibility of gender diverse people, predominantly, social categories in Western society are dichotomous with recognition as a citizen of either male or female sex/gender. Consider the most fundamental system to which most people belong: the family. Available roles within families are designated by gender: mother, father, son, daughter, auntie and so on. Gaining recognition within these binary categories results in both gains and losses for trans populations (Sanger, 2010). This is particularly so at the junctures of 'coming out' and transitioning (the process of changing gender) as the costs of both can be catastrophic in terms of personal, social and economic loss. Some examples include estrangement from family, hate crimes and the loss of employment.

Citizenship and trans communities

There is a general consensus that the notion of citizenship pertains to social, political and civic rights, but Plummer (1995) argues that 'intimate citizenship' rights becomes a fourth aspect. His analysis is mostly anchored to sexuality and individual choice, but he briefly considers trans people as a gender and sexual minority and includes the principle of freedom to determine one's own gender identity. The specific issue of trans people's rights and citizenship has been taken up by various authors in recent years and, overall, Plummer's attention to personal choice concurs with Monro's (2005) discussion of trans citizenship which is concerned with self-determination and equity (Monro and Warren, 2004; Monro, 2005; Hines, 2013). While analyses of gender and citizenship are not new, the issues for trans people's rights can be distinguished from feminist concerns which are rooted to the gender binary and women's inequality. In addition, trans people's citizenship differs, in terms of needs and rights, from Plummer's model of intimate citizenship which primarily focuses on sexual desire and intimacy. Grabham (2007) claims that there is a tension between these three models of citizenship (intimate, feminist and trans) with each attempting to delineate their own specificity.

As trans citizenship has been allied to a rights-based approach, Monro (2005: 166) points out the limitations of rights-oriented models which '[...] simply mean a replication of the dominant order, or assimilation of marginalised groups into the mainstream'. For some members of the trans population, however, and particularly those who identify as transsexual, assimilation into mainstream society *is* the desired goal. So there is a congruence with the generic citizenship model, which incorporates social, political and civic rights and is grounded in a heteronormative socio-cultural context. Ideally, therefore, the model could be broadened to include the trans perspective. However, this broadening requires complex legal reconfiguration and while legislative change has taken place (for example, with the implementation of the Gender Recognition Act 2004 and the Equality Act 2010 – see below), this is far from complete (Sandland, 2005; Sharpe, 2007).

In addition, there is a faction of the trans population who do not wish to conform to male or female identities and as 'gender outlaws' – a description to signify gender transgression in the context of identity, practice and social status – they reject conventional and universal citizenship rights (Bornstein, 1998). This also problematises notions of trans citizenship, as trans people's rights have increasingly come to mean transsexual rights with advocacy within the community itself focusing on issues such as hate crimes towards transsexuals and access to medical intervention; these are of interest mostly to those who wish to reassign their sex (those who practice and identify within the gender binary) (Wilchins, 2004). Clearly making claims for a single model of trans citizenship, along with the development of social policy to support such a model, is convoluted and problematic.

Working within the field of citizenship studies, Tee and Hegarty (2006) explored public support and opposition to the civil rights of trans people in the UK. The study found there to be more opposition to trans civil rights among 'men … non-White, non-British, religious, authoritarian and heterosexist participants and those with little previous contact with gender minorities' (Tee and Hegarty, 2006: 77). There were differences in prejudice towards sexual and gender minorities, but the researchers found that there was no predictable correlation between the two, nor was prejudice based on conceptual confusion of the two groups. Tee and Hegarty (2006: 78) suggest that 'both prejudices might be rooted in right wing authoritarian acceptance of, and reliance on, authority to punish those who transgress social norms'. While these findings are cogent and indicate some ways of contextualising the trans perspective of marginalisation, the study sample was modest. In addition, although attitudes and beliefs were measured, behaviours or behavioural intentions (such as hate crime) were not. The findings do, however, support existing research which suggests widespread disadvantage for trans populations (Whittle et al., 2007; Mitchell and Howarth, 2009). These findings also suggest that more needs to be done to enable trans people to exercise their citizenship rights on an equal footing with their cisgender counterparts. However, Monro (2003) has pointed out that trans people are underrepresented in decision-making processes, creating a further barrier to full inclusion.

The problem of trans inequality has not gone unnoticed in the UK, as in July 2015 the Women and Equalities Committee announced that it was to embark on an inquiry. This will consider how far, and in what ways, trans people still have yet to achieve full equality and to determine how the issues can most effectively be addressed. Committee Chair Maria Miller said:

> Many trans people still face discrimination and unfair treatment in their work, schools, healthcare and other important services. Transphobia and hate crimes are a cruel reminder that we still have a great deal to do to achieve true equality for everyone. I hope that trans people will feel able to share their experiences with our inquiry, so that the committee can make recommendations for improving people's lives. (Women and Equalities Committee, 2015: online)

The government has previously tried to address trans inequality through the 'Transgender Equality Plan' 2011. However, evidence indicates that the marginalisation and discrimination of trans people continues as it does across Europe and the globe, as trans people are still disproportionally affected by discrimination in all areas of life, for example in education, employment, public transportation or access to goods and services (TGEU, 2015a: online).

The policy framework

In the context of trans citizenship and equality there have been advancements made, notably, with the introduction of the Gender Recognition Act (GRA) 2004. The GRA provides a mechanism to enable trans people to obtain recognition for all legal purposes in their preferred gender identity via the acquisition of a Gender Recognition Certificate (GRC). An application for a GRC has to be made to a Gender Recognition Panel. There is a standard route to obtaining a GRC which stipulates that the applicant is 18 or over; has been diagnosed with gender dysphoria; has been living in their acquired gender in the UK for at least two years; and intends to live in their acquired gender for the remainder of their life (HM Government, 2015). There is an alternative route which reflects the changes incurred following the Marriage (Same Sex Couples) Act 2013. For trans people who are married, the Marriage (Same Sex Couples) Act 2013 enables their transition on obtaining a GRC, as their existing marriage can be converted to a same-sex or different sex marriage as appropriate. This replaces the previous condition that a trans person must divorce before applying for a GRC. This conversion does, however, require the consent of the non-trans person.

The GRA represents the civil recognition of trans-identified people and confers rights such as the ability to obtain a new birth certificate and the possibility to marry in one's acquired gender. Importantly, the Act removed the legal recognition of 'sex' from the requirement to have surgical intervention, bringing a new framework for understanding the relationship between the concepts of sex and gender (Hines, 2013). In addition, the GRA addresses welfare and employment by offering protection to trans people who obtain a GRC by removing the requirement for trans people to reveal their former gender identity to professional bodies. It offers protection in terms of privacy by including a clause which means that it is unlawful for a public official to reveal a person's trans status to another individual or agency (with some minor exceptions).

Reflection
_____

Under s.22(4) of the Gender Recognition Act any public official (for example, a healthcare worker, or social worker) should not reveal a person's trans status or former gender identity without the express permission of the individual.

How do you think this applies to health and social care workers who may have had to deal with sensitive issues?

In the UK trans people are also conferred rights under the Equality Act 2010, as 'gender reassignment' is one of the nine protected characteristics. In this context, gender reassignment refers to anyone whose gender identity differs from the gender assigned to them at birth. Some writers suggest that the Equality Act 2010, and legislative change in general, is evidence of a changing social climate and subsequently a shift in cultural norms. In fact, the Equality Act 2010 is indicative of a trajectory in social attitudes and perspectives on trans which moves from a medical to a social discourse, as within the act itself it is stipulated that gender reassignment is to be considered to be a social, not medical, process. The Equality and Human Rights Commission clarify this point by stating:

> To be protected from gender reassignment discrimination, you do not need to have undergone any specific treatment or surgery to change from your birth sex to your preferred gender. This is because changing your physiological or other gender attributes is a personal process rather than a medical one. You can be at any stage in the transition process – from proposing to reassign your gender, to undergoing a process to reassign your gender, or having completed it. (EHRC, 2015: online)

However, the limitations of gauging social change through the prism of legislation requires a critical understanding of how the gender binary undergirds equality legislation and consequently neglects trans people who identify outside of the male/female gender binary. Therefore, the Gender Recognition Act 2014 and the Equality Act 2010 are only partially responsive to the human rights and citizenship demands of trans people.

As noted above, during 2015 the Women and Equalities Committee led an inquiry on behalf of Parliament into trans equality, and a review of policy and legislation formed just one aspect of this. In relation to the GRA, questions have been raised about the bureaucratic nature of the processes of gender recognition as well as procedures being too expensive and overly medicalised. Advocates of and for the trans community have raised questions about whether trans people in the UK should be able to define their gender as the law allows in other countries such as Denmark or Ireland where gender is not confined to a binary identification (Saner, 2014). Overall, however, in terms of legal gender recognition the European context is piecemeal:

> The Council of Europe demands that its member states provide for legal gender recognition, but only 35 countries in Europe do so, and only 1 currently does not demand that trans people undergo sterilisation or medical interventions, divorce, or a psychological diagnosis or assessment. These abusive requirements, or the lack of legislation altogether, means that most trans people are stuck with documents that do not match their gender identity. (TGEU, 2015c: online)

It is these types of issues that are being reviewed by the UK's trans inquiry as 'the Committee is aware that full equality for trans people still has not been achieved. In its inquiry the Committee is looking at a range of outstanding issues and considering how they can most effectively be addressed' (the Women and Equalities Committee, 2015: online).

Reflection

The trans equality inquiry will look at a range of processes and phenomena as well as levels of social exclusion and discrimination (for example, current legislation, hate crime and the recording of information in official documentation).

Considering the discussion so far in this chapter, what do you think should be the priority for the inquiry? What is your reasoning?

Key issues for practice: barriers and challenges in practice contexts

Societal attitudes are generally reflected within health and social care services, and, as transphobia and gender normativity are pervasive in the wider world, they may also permeate practice contexts, affecting trans people's experiences of and access to health and social care. Indeed, Somerville (2015) asserts that in an in-depth survey which explored lesbian, gay, bisexual and trans (LGBT) issues in health and social care contexts, one in five respondents reported to have heard negative comments made about trans people. Moreover, many trans people experience a considerable amount of transphobia and harassment in their day-to-day lives, and may come to expect it from services too. All these experiences are potential barriers to trans people even contemplating accessing health and/or social care services. People who identify as non-binary face additional challenges, as most services will require their service users to ascribe to one gender or the other. For example, forms and other documents often require a person to tick a box as 'M' or 'F'; other gender identities cease to exist.

Commonly, trans people have an ambivalent relationship to medicine and the healthcare profession in the context of achieving social and personal recognition; on the one hand, recognising the need for medical interventions (such as hormones, or reassignment surgery), and on the other, resisting the over-medicalisation of their lived experience (Couch et al., 2008). In relation to social care and social work, however, there is little evidence to explore the relationship between the profession and trans populations, as the latter remain largely invisible as service users of social care (Mitchell and Howarth 2009; Rogers, 2013). Barriers to accessing services are various but include concerns of being routed through misgendering practices (for example, people using the incorrect pronouns) through to the fear of discrimination and being refused access on the grounds of gender identity and presentation (Whittle et al., 2007).

Case study: **barriers and challenges in practice contexts**

Between the years 2011 and 2012 a qualitative research study was conducted which explored trans people's experiences of domestic violence and abuse (DVA), their resulting social care needs and any interaction with social care services. Rogers (2013) interviewed 15 people whose ages ranged from 21 to 70. Participants self-identified in binary and non-binary ways, including as trans, transgender, transsexual; as having a transsexual history; as queer; and as genderqueer.

None of the participants had approached a social care provider or a specialist DVA agency (for example, refuge accommodation) but a small number had experienced contact with social care professionals for other reasons. These varied in terms of positive and negative experience. Social work student Max (aged 25) held a strong opinion about social care and social work services that employed eligibility criteria which primarily centred on gender. Max shared a very personal account about his experiences of undergoing counselling to address childhood experiences of sexual abuse:

> Before starting counselling [at a rape crisis centre], I wrote to the service manager explaining that I identified as genderqueer, which is how I identified at the time, and that I did not identify as female. Despite that fact I was allowed to access the service, until the point where I told my counsellor I was getting top surgery (breast removal). The next week I was told that my 18-month counselling contract was being cut short to around 3 months (leaving us with one more session), as I was 'becoming a man', and may start to make the women accessing the service feel threatened. I feel like the

service manager took an entirely essentialist approach to my gender identity, and that the decision of whether or not I was (too) male and therefore, in the service manager's eyes, a potential threat to other service users was based on my body – specifically, my chest – rather than the whole package of me as a person.

I do understand the desire and need for 'women's only' spaces (where they include trans women), and it is therefore not the fact that I was excluded from this service which has undermined my opinion of this and other similar services. What has led to my negative perception of this service is the way in which I was suddenly dropped as a service user, when I was at a point in my life where I was at risk of suicide due to the upcoming trial of the man who abused me. The service manager's decision … felt incredibly negligent and discriminatory, and has damaged my trust in … services' commitment to providing support to trans and other gender variant people.

Based on my personal and professional experiences and other anecdotal experiences I've come across … I do not feel that the agencies providing this [social care] support are yet at a point where they are willing and committed to engaging with trans people and learning about what type of support we need and providing it. I think that currently the status quo is to provide the legal minimum of services: [for example] services will only be provided to women who have a Gender Recognition Certificate and have changed their birth certificate. Any … agency which supports that type of policy is not committed to providing equal services to all.

This case study clearly shows how Max's treatment was underpinned by a complex intersection of stereotypical attitudes in combination with a lack of understanding about gender identity and trans embodiment. Max pointed to the way that some social problems (such as DVA and sexual violence) are seen to be gendered in ways that are problematic for trans and non-binary people like Max. This is indicative of heteronormativity and gender normativity, but, in addition, Max alludes to the problems that the legal and policy framework creates for practice when this framework employs a particular way of categorising trans people to fit with existing social structures, and thus excludes a section of this population. This highlights a challenge for practice in terms of working with the Other, or as Max termed it 'dealing with the unknown'.

A barrier to effective service provision, then, is the tendency to signpost trans (and other minority people) on to other 'specialist' services, illustrating a common-found reluctance of mainstream providers to offer services before they feel adequately trained/experienced/knowledgeable. Service providers may also wish to avoid tokenism. Alternatively, specialist providers, such as DVA services, can feel confident that their responses to minority people will be as competent as with any other service user, as the central focus is upon the specialist issue not the individual's social characteristics (Rogers, 2013, 2015). Yet it is important to acknowledge the range of barriers resulting from the intersection of trans identity and other social characteristics such as ethnicity, age, socio-economic class, mental health status, age and disability. Signposting trans people to specialist LGBT services may provide expert support to trans people, but they may not be much help to trans people who are experiencing racism, disablism or ageism.

In terms of the perceptions and knowledge of practitioners in health and social care, a lack of available training, or the problem of undertaking training which is not then applied in practice, can lead to limited awareness in terms of the specific risks and issues that affect trans people. For example, trans people who are undertaking hormone replacement therapy can experience highly unstable emotional states if they are not prescribed the correct dosage. Similarly, 'due to continuous experiences of discrimination and social exclusion, trans people tend to have poorer mental and physical health than the overall population, in part because access to medical care is difficult or impossible' (TGEU, 2015b: online). These types of issues are easily missed, misinterpreted or misunderstood by health and social care practitioners who are unable to recognise and assess risk accurately. Likewise, the process of making informed decisions about trans people and their lives is limited without some awareness of trans issues. Moreover, there can often be a pathologising focus on the individual in health and social care, with less attention being paid to the associated socio-cultural, environmental and/or material factors (for example, limited access to social networks, or lack of money due to unemployment). This pathologising approach can overlook the reasons why trans people might have difficulties in accessing health and social care services, and therefore it is unlikely to offer helpful solutions such as tackling transphobia in everyday life or exploring other pathways for help to progress gender transitioning.

Messages for health and social care providers

Within the context of health and social care provision, tackling entrenched and systemic issues such as heteronormativity, gender normativity and cisgenderism is a complex task. These concepts could, however, help to critically examine whether or not contemporary policy and practice promotes trans equality and inclusion. Yet, due to the dearth of literature and a modest evidence base, it is difficult to determine this one way or another. This is further exacerbated by the suggestion that trans people are not easily identified as service users (Mitchell and Howarth, 2009; Rogers, 2013, 2015). When research is undertaken which explores the interface of health and social care services with trans populations, unfortunately there are some gaps in terms of knowledge and expertise (Somerville, 2015). Notwithstanding, across the sectors of health, social care and social work there are overlapping discourses and ethics that hold potential to counter these gaps. These values, discourses and practices include the concepts of 'care', 'social justice' and 'equity' (BASW, 2012).

In terms of the everyday, organisations should develop visible campaigns to deter transphobic bullying and harassment (Somerville, 2015) and practitioners could engage in awareness training around trans identity and practice but also in terms of improving trans-inclusion and equality. The participants in Rogers' (2013) study felt that this commitment could be incorporated into policy and protocols so that a 'trans friendly' or 'trans positive' quality mark could be adopted by a health or social care provider to show itself to be a learning organisation. Consequently, this would also demonstrate to trans people a commitment towards the community through the attitudes and training of its staff. In addition, participants advocated the development of a narrative model to practice in order to facilitate a person-centred approach to understanding life stories and the individual in their environment. Some interpersonal micro-practices (such as the use of correct pronouns and titles) would indicate genuine person-centredness and positive regard to individual service users in a way that structural and systemic change cannot. On a practical note, organisational efforts towards demonstrating trans inclusion are also easily achieved: for example, paying attention to daily care practices (providing service users with gender appropriate facilities or items).

Conclusion

The potential of legislative change means that trans people have greater levels of legal redress, and therefore personal agency, within the contexts of both personal and public life. However, the premise that trans people benefit from increasing recognition enabled, to some degree, through legislation and policy is contested, as the legislative framework does not recognise the diversity of trans identities and practices. This is particularly true for people who do not identify within a binary understanding of gender. Thus, trans people continue to experience high levels of marginalisation and comparatively lower levels of citizenship (Hines, 2013). In addition, policy is yet to be effective in recognising and tackling trans people's lived experiences, which includes public hate crime, harassment and widespread discrimination (Whittle et al. 2007; the Women and Equalities Committee, 2015). The continuing challenges for inclusive practice in health and social care can overwhelmingly be seen as rooted in the existing frameworks (in terms of citizenship, gender, policy and practice) which are underpinned by heteronormative, gender normative and cisgenderist biases. This chapter has explored these challenges and suggested some strategies to increase trans inclusion in health and social care and these, ultimately, help to further an understanding of what it means to be a 'trans ally' (PFLAG National, 2014).

Recommended reading

- Hines, S. (2013) *Gender Diversity, Recognition and Citizenship: Towards a Politics of Difference.* Basingstoke: Palgrave Macmillan

- Monro, S. (2005) *Gender Politics: Citizenship, Activism and Sexual Diversity.* London: Pluto Press.

- Serano, J. (2013) *Excluded: Making Feminist and Queer Movements More Inclusive.* Berkeley: Seal Press.

Relevant web links

- **www.mermaidsuk.org.uk** Mermaids is a charity which offers family and individual support for teenagers and children with gender identity issues

- **www.equalityhumanrights.com** The Equality and Human Rights Commission states 'we live in a country with a long history of upholding people's rights, valuing diversity and challenging intolerance. The EHRC seeks to maintain and strengthen this heritage while identifying and tackling areas where there is still unfair discrimination or where human rights are not being respected.'

- **http://tgeu.org/** Transgender Europe (TGEU) is a human rights organisation working towards the full equality for all trans people in Europe.

- **www.gires.org.uk** GIRES (Gender Identity and Research Society) is a voluntary sector charity that, in collaboration with the other groups in its field, hears, helps, empowers and gives a voice to trans and gender non-conforming individuals, including those who are non-binary and non-gender, as well as their families. GIRES contributes to policy development and delivering training.

References

Ansara, Y.G. and Hegarty, P. (2011) Cisgenderism in psychology: pathologising and misgendering children from 1999 to 2008. *Psychology & Sexuality* iFirst, 1–24. Available at: www.tandfonline.com/doi/abs/10.1080/19419899.2011.576696 (accessed 26 June 2016).

Aoki, R. (2012) When something is not right. In A. Enke (ed.) *Transfeminist Perspectives in and Beyond Transgender and Gender Studies.* Pennsylvania: Temple University Press.

BASW (2012) *The Code of Ethics for Social Workers: Statement of Principles.* Birmingham: BASW.

Blumer, M.L.C., Ansara, Y.G. and Watson, C.M. (2013) Cisgenderism in family therapy: how everyday clinical practices can delegitimize people's gender self-designations. *Journal of Family Psychotherapy* 24: 267–285.

Bornstein, K. (1998) *Gender Outlaw: On Men, Women and the Rest of Us.* London: Routledge.

Butler, J. (1990) *Gender Trouble: Feminism and the Subversion of Identity.* New York: Routledge.

_____(2004) *Undoing Gender.* New York: Routledge.

Chakraborti, N. and Hardy, S. (2015) LGB&T Hate Crime Reporting: Identifying Barriers and Solutions. Manchester: Equality and Human Rights Commission.

Couch, M., Pitts, M.K., Croy, S., Mulcare, H. and Mitchell, A. (2008) Transgender people and the amendment of formal documentation: matters of recognition and citizenship. *Health Sociology Review,* 17(3): 280–289.

Davy, Z. (2011) *Recognizing Transsexuals: Personal, Political and Medicolegal Embodiment.* Farnham: Ashgate.

EHRC ((2015) *Gender Reassignment Discrimination.* Available at: www.equalityhuman rights.com/your-rights/equal-rights/gender-reassignment-discrimination (accessed 11 December 2015).

Enke, A. (2012) *Transfeminist Perspectives In and Beyond Transgender and Queer Studies.* Philadelphia: Temple University Press.

Fausto-Sterling, A. (2000) *Sexing the Body: Gender Politics and the Construction of Sexuality.* New York: Basic Books.

Gamson, J. (1998) *Freaks Talk Back: Tabloid Talk Shows and Sexual Nonconformity.* Chicago: University of Chicago Press.

Garfinkel, H. (1967) *Studies in Ethnomethodology.* Cambridge: Polity Press.

Grabham, E. (2007) Citizen bodies, intersex citizenship. *Sexualities,* 10(1): 29–48.

Hines, S. (2007) (Trans)forming gender: Social change and transgender citizenship. *Sociological Research Online,* 12(1). Available at: www.socresonline.org.uk/12/1/hines.html (accessed 26 June 2016).

_____(2013) *Gender Diversity, Recognition and Citizenship: Towards a Politics of Difference.* Basingstoke: Palgrave Macmillan.

HM Government (2015) *Applying for Gender Recognition Certificate.* Available at: www.gov.uk/apply-gender-recognition-certificate (accessed 10 October 2015).

Iantaffi, A. and Bockting, W.O. (2011) Views from both sides of the bridge? Gender, sexual legitimacy and transgender people's experiences of relationships. *Culture, Health and Sexuality* 13(3): 355–370.

Kennedy, N. (2013) Cultural cisgenderism: consequences of the imperceptible. *Psychology of Women Section Review* 15(2): 1–7.

Mitchell, M. and Howarth, C. (2009) *Trans Research Review.* Manchester: Equality and Human Rights Commission.

Monro, S. (2003) Transgender politics in the UK. *Critical Social Policy,* 23(4): 433–452.

_____(2005) *Gender Politics: Citizenship, Activism and Sexual Diversity.* London: Pluto Press.

_____(2007) Transmuting gender binaries: the theoretical challenge. *Sociological Research Online* 12(1). Available at: www.socresonline.org.uk/12/1/monro.html (accessed 13 January 2015).

Monro, S. and Warren, L. (2004) Transgendering citizenship. *Sexualities*, 7(3): 345–362.

O'Keefe, T. (1999) *Sex, Gender and Sexuality: 21st Century Transformations*. London: Extraordinary People Press.

PFLAG National (2014) *The Guide to Being a Trans Ally*. Washington DC: PFLAG National.

Plummer, K. (1995) *Telling Sexual Stories: Power, Change and Social Worlds*. London: Routledge

Prosser, J. (1998) *Second Skins: The Body Narratives of Transsexuality*. New York: Columbia University Press.

Rogers, M. (2013) *TransForming Practice: Understanding Trans People's Experience of Domestic Abuse and Social Care Agencies*. PhD thesis, University of Sheffield, UK.

_____(2015) Breaking down barriers: exploring the potential for social care practice with trans survivors of domestic abuse. *Health and Social Care in the Community*. Epub ahead of print 9 February 2015. DOI: 10.1111/hsc.12193.

_____(2016) Transphobic 'honour'-based abuse: a conceptual tool. *Sociology*. Available at: http://soc.sagepub.com/content/early/2016/01/12/0038038515622907.full.pdf? ijkey=RoGzkZLYExDY9HL&keytype=finite (accessed 20 January 2016).

Sandland, R. (2005) Feminism and the Gender Recognition Act 2004. *Feminist Legal Studies*, 13: 43–66.

Saner, E. (2014) Europe's terrible trans track record: will Denmark's new law spark change? *The Guardian*, 1 September 2014. Available at: www.theguardian.com/ society/shortcuts/2014/sep/01/europe-terrible-trans-rights-record-denmark-new-law (accessed 12/11/2015).

Sanger, T. (2010) *Trans People's Partnership: Towards an Ethics of Intimacy*. Basingstoke: Palgrave Macmillan.

Sedgwick, E. (1990) *Epistemology of the Closet*. Berkeley: University of California Press.

Serano, J. (2007) *Whipping Girl: A Transsexual Woman on Sexism and the Scapegoating of Femininity*. Berkeley: Seal Press.

_____(2013) *Excluded: Making Feminist and Queer Movements More Inclusive*. Berkley: Seal Press.

Sharpe, A. (2007) Endless sex: the Gender Recognition Act 2004 and the persistence of a legal category. *Feminist Legal Studies*, 15: 57–84.

Somerville, C. (2015) *Unhealthy Attitudes: The Treatment of LGBT People within Health and Social Care Services*. London: Stonewall.

Stryker, S. and Aizura, A. (2013) *The Transgender Studies Reader 2*. New York: Routledge.

Tee, N. and Hegarty, P. (2006) Predicting opposition to the civil rights of trans persons in the United Kingdom. *Journal of Community and Applied Social Psychology*, 16: 70–80.

Valentine, D. (2007) The calculus of pain: violence, anthropological ethics and the category transgender. *Ethnos*, 68: 27–48.

TGEU (2015a) *Non-Discrimination*. Available at: http://tgeu.org/issues/discrimination/ (accessed 12/11/2015).

_____(2015b) *General Health*. Available at: http://tgeu.org/issues/health_and_ depathologisation/general-health/ (accessed 12/11/2015).

_____(2015c) *Legal Gender Recognition*. Available at: http://tgeu.org/issues/legal-gender-recognition/ (accessed 12/11/2015).

Warner, M. (ed.) (1991) *Fear of a Queer Planet*. Minneapolis MN: University of Minnesota Press.

Whittle, S., Turner, L. and Al-Alami, M. (2007) *Engendered Penalties: Transgender and Transsexual People's Experiences of Inequality and Discrimination*. Wetherby: Crown and Local Government Publications.

Wilchins, R. (2004) *Queer Theory, Gender Theory: An Instant Primer*. Los Angeles: Alyson Publications.

Women and Equalities Committee (2015) *Transgender equality inquiry launched*. Available at: www.parliament.uk/business/committees/committees-a-z/commons-select/women-and-equalities-committee/news-parliament-2015/inquiry-into-transgender-equality/ (accessed 10 October 2015).

7

DEAFNESS AND SOCIAL EXCLUSION

Naomi Sharples and Will Hough

Chapter overview: **key messages**

- Deaf people have experienced degrees of exclusion from the mainstream of society for millennia.
- This exclusion exerts great pressure on individuals, their family relationships, educational attainment, employment and health.
- Equalising access to society's institutions is the most empowering of all acts that individuals, both Deaf and hearing, can achieve because increased inclusion supports better education, employment and healthy lives.

Introduction

This chapter will outline and explore how Deaf people's marginalisation and difficulties in accessing health and social care are determined by historical and current institutional contexts. The chapter identifies how communication through spoken language is the fundamental platform to accessing family, education and quality healthcare provision. The chapter uses case studies to illustrate the impact of Deafness upon an individual's life and highlights how the mitigating actions of healthcare practitioners can remove barriers and improve people's experiences of services and quality of life.

Historical context

When using the term 'Deaf' (with a capital D) we are not referring to the 10 million people whose deafness is a result of old age or industrial injury or who are defined as 'hard of hearing'. We are referring to the 60–70,000 people who are profoundly deaf and those who prefer to use a shared signed language and who live within the Deaf Community; although it must be fully acknowledged that all people with hearing loss and deafness (with a small d) may have similar experiences of social exclusion.

Deafness is not a contemporary societal problem; the social exclusion experienced by Deaf people has been documented as far back as 1000BC where Hebrew law was enshrined which denied Deaf people the right to own land or to marry. In the early 1500s the development of a signed language was recognised within the European upper classes; this was instigated due to the number of Deaf children born to landed gentry and their need to inherit. Groce (1988) gives an insight into the 1690s and how, in the small island community of Martha's Vineyard, Deaf people were treated as equals among their peers because they made up 1:4 of the population. In this context, inclusion was established by everyone learning to sign because it was the islanders' natural way to communicate. With the establishment of large Schools for Deaf Children on the mainland and the resulting dispersal of the island's Deaf population, this community and their shared language became history.

Seventeenth century Western society saw educators, such as Johann Amman and Henry Baker, begin to specialise in teaching lip-reading as an educational method. This provided a level of social acceptance that came with having a 'voice'; this was motivated by a belief that this was the deaf child's only way to know God (Ree, 1999). This oral system was supported by scientist/inventor and eugenicist Dr Alexander Graham Bell (1847–1922), who advocated the movement away from sign language, and this included his drive to ensure Deaf people did not marry.

In 1880 at the 2nd International Congress on Education of the Deaf in Milan, Italy, it was voted to embrace the use of oral education of Deaf people and for sign language to be 'removed' from schools. This included the removal of children's teachers who were Deaf and with this removal children were quickly without Deaf adult role models. Children were now 'taught' to speak using any limited hearing they may have and an array of exercises and techniques. Most children would spend about half of their education learning speech. Some of the methods used constituted abuse: for example, ducking the child's head in a bowl of water if the child was not expelling air correctly. It took a further 130 years to re-establish sign language in the education system, supported by the recognition of British Sign Language as a native British language in 2003 by the then Labour Government. In Britain today there are a variety of approaches to Deaf children's education, including oral, signed and total communication (using all possible input channels to develop language skills); each method is only as useful as it is accessible for the child and only as good as the educator supporting the child.

The oppression D/deaf people have experienced over the centuries can shed light on the contemporary position Deaf people experience in relation to the disability debate. Often people view Deafness as a disability, impairment or handicap and these negative views are more disabling to the person than the physical inability to hear (Meadows-Orlans and Erting, 2000). There are reports of hearing parents of Deaf children entering into a grieving process when informed of their child's deafness; the loss experienced by the parents can be significant. Social media abounds with triumph over tragedy tales of Deaf children hearing for the first time and Health Services continue to offer cochlear implants (electronic hearing aids implanted directly into the cochlear) in an attempt to restore the child's hearing, with little choice offered for the child to choose to be Deaf or Deaf with an implanted hearing aid. Our society is bound to an image of normalcy where Deafness is presented as something needing to be 'cured'.

Geneticists continue to work on the 'Deaf Gene'. This hereditary factor affects 5 per cent of the Deaf population. Deaf people with a familial link are seen as the carriers of language and culture for many Deaf community members and yet the scientists want to eradicate the gene. Members of this minority group share a language, experiences and culture; they are proud to be different; they are proud to be Deaf. In British society there has been a low-profile debate ensuing between those who consider Deafness a disability and those who do not.

While the authors of this chapter are aligned with the concept of Deaf people belonging to a linguistic and cultural minority, it is very clear that others do not hold the same position. Therefore, it is necessary to explain the linguistic/cultural position because some people understand the concept of deafness from purely a medical/normalcy paradigm.

Models that help understand d/Deafness

At a basic level we are offered the medical versus the social positions in regard to disability. First, we are presented with the term 'disabled' or 'disability' as the individual's 'deficit' position, where the disability is attributed to the individual. This is credited to the medical/pathological model of disability (Giddens, 2006). Second, the social model of disability takes the position that disability is forced onto the individual not because of what the individual can or cannot do, rather it is driven by society and the resulting environment's inability to include the individual who, for example, uses a wheelchair, or who is d/Deaf. However, there is a desire among some disability writers to move away from deficit models and to challenge the model of 'normalcy' (Davis, 1995). This narrow position of 'normalcy' that values particular bodies, ideals and beliefs over others, they argue, is a stifling and politically elitist position. Devaluing 'normalcy' would awaken society's understanding of the beauty and complexity of disability as well as the vast wealth of knowledge and strength of consciousness that disabled people have, which, due to the value placed on 'normates', is an untapped human resource (Davis, 2002).

Some Deaf people may see themselves as different from disabled people; many Deaf people have no sense of wanting to be 'cured' or treated for their deafness. Here Deaf people align themselves to the medical model, mistakenly believing that all disabled people want to be made 'better', as exemplified by Adams and Rohring (2004) who argue that some Deaf people 'adopt the alien disability construct' (Adams and Rohring, 2004: 139). As such these people promulgate the negative values placed on disabled individuals believing that because they are content with their linguistic, cultural and auditory status then they should not be classified as 'disabled'; thus reinforcing the concept of disability as a deficit position.

The State acknowledges that due to society's disabling nature, people require funding to support their access to the world. For example, Deaf students' access is funded through the Disabled Student Allowance (DSA). The Equality Act (2010) supports students in their access to higher education. If one was to take the position of believing Deaf people are from a linguistic minority group, accessing disability funding may appear disingenuous, and unfair to the other students for whom English is not their first language. For Deaf students there may be gains in relation to written English; however, gains in spoken English will be limited according to the availability of language therapy (Barnes, 2007), their need, choice and ability to speak. As such there will always be a reliance on human and technical resources to make the education environment accessible, which is different to the needs of foreign students who would require language classes and support for a limited amount of time depending on their skills.

The important issue for the d/Deaf student is that DSA covers their needs. As such, d/Deaf people and hearing educators will utilise the resources available to them because, they argue, despite challenging the medical/deficit model of deafness promulgated by society and supported through legislation, with no alternative available they have to resort to accepting support that is determined by society and its institutions.

Deaf people have challenged the disability movement by denying their disability; in contrast, the disability rights movement aligns with the discourse of the dominant majority by including Deaf people in the disability framework (Obassi cited in Barnes, 2007). Language is at the crux of the issue: one language shared by the majority including disabled people compared to sign language used by people from the deaf community. In the past Deaf activists have called for deaf-only areas, services and the acknowledgement of an international Deaf community uniting Deaf people throughout the world (Branson and Miller, 2002).

Hearing people who see Deaf people as disabled are unlikely to find themselves in the midst of a discussion about Deaf identity or the structure of society. Therefore, the debate remains within the community and has little impact on the wider society. As Obassi (2007) concludes, unless academics take their debates from within the deaf community to the generic arena they will remain outside the grand narrative and there will be a constant need for researchers to reiterate and re-narrate the 'deaf' versus 'Deaf' and deaf versus disabled/disability debate.

Drawing on the notion that knowledge and information offer freedom and emancipation, when deaf people find themselves outside the disability debate this is often due to the lack of shared language. Disabled people use the language of the majority, and this creates difference immediately. Until a real understanding of the role of a shared and accessible language is fully understood as the most significant issue that disbars and disables some deaf people from society and society's institutions the deafness versus disability debate will continue.

Legislation and policy

Within the last 20 years we have seen policies and legislation introduced to improve the access to health and social care in the UK. Prior to 1995 the legislation and policy introduced to support Deaf people was focused around access to education and employment. In 1997 a Social Inspectorate Report – 'Service on the Edge' – identified that services for Deaf people were below acceptable standards in terms of assessment and communication and offered guidance on how best to meet the needs of Deaf people; the follow - up report in 1999 – 'Stepping Away from the Edge' – offered further guidance to social services in the provision of care for Deaf people. 'The Sign of the Times' (2002) and 'Towards Equity and Access' (TEA) reports (2005) were triggered by a homicide inquiry and designed to improve Deaf people's access to mental healthcare services. The reports triggered the improvement of assertive outreach, inpatient and outpatient service availability for Deaf adults and children requiring mental healthcare services.

For all health and social care services the introduction of the Disability Discrimination Act (1995) saw a change to the provision of services for Deaf people. Although many Deaf people do not see their Deafness as a disability, the DDA (1995) clearly covered 'physical or mental impairment which has a substantial and long term adverse effect on their ability to carry out normal day to day activities'. The changes to the law giving Deaf people the rights to have 'reasonable adjustments' in the workplace and the access to goods, facilities and services resulted in changes to how health and social care services acted upon the needs of Deaf people; for example, having to wait longer for a service on account of your disability was no longer an acceptable reason.

The Human Rights Act (1998) identified a number of fundamental rights for Deaf people which did not require to be earned but ensured the right to live with dignity, in freedom, in a safe environment where people respect each other without fear of discrimination; for example, failure to provide a deaf person with communication support or sign language interpreter within the public sector (court/hospital) would be a breach of article 14 (non-discrimination), and in terms of the court article 6 (rights to a fair trial).

The Equality Act (2010) combines and replaces previous discrimination legislation, including the DDA (1995); therefore, if a person met the requirements under the DDA (1995) they would be covered by the Equality Act (2010), which identifies protected characteristics such as age, disability, gender reassignment, marriage and civil partnerships, pregnancy and maternity, race, religion or belief, sex and sexual orientation. This includes the direct and indirect discrimination of Deaf people witnessed by society, and discrimination hearing children with Deaf parents witness as they associate with someone who is Deaf or mistakenly believed to be Deaf. Despite legislation it comes as no surprise that there are few complaints or legal challenges to the exclusion from services Deaf people experience. This lack of action is not a result of all services meeting the requirements to make themselves, but more likely a result of the oppression Deaf people have endured over the years and reluctance to raise complaints: disempowered individuals are not always the best complainants.

Deaf people's access to healthcare

Deaf people report positive and negative experiences when accessing health and social care services. Positive experiences or satisfaction with the care and treatment they receive are usually found when Deaf people have accessed services that have utilised appropriately trained sign language interpreters or the professionals they engage with are suitably qualified in BSL (Heslop and Turnbull, 2013). However, these positive experiences are significantly outweighed by the negative reports, with several areas of difficulty in not only accessing services but also the inability to benefit from services or utilise treatments available.

Deaf people often avoid health and social care services due to fear, mistrust and frustration (Kritzinger, Schneider, Swartz and Braathen, 2014). This can lead to problems with early prevention and severe physical or mental health conditions going untreated. The GP Patient survey (2011) in England, however, identified that Deaf adults use primary care services more than the general population; albeit 44 per cent of those who responded reported 'a difficult' or 'very difficult' experience on their last visit to the GP. We should not presume that the issue with health and social care is only within the service; problems are often observed even before the Deaf person makes the appointment, with 40 per cent reporting issues with receptionists being 'unhelpful' or 'very unhelpful' when trying to book appointments. Deaf people reported attending but missing their appointment because they were 'called' for by the professional who failed to notice they were Deaf.

The main reported problems for access to services are the issues around communication and failure of the communication strategies identified previously. Other issues include professionals having no insight or knowledge of the Deaf community and their culture, or the additional physical or cognitive complications linked to organic causes of Deafness.

Deaf people's access to psychiatric services

Hindley and Kitson (2000) state Deaf people have a higher prevalence for mental illness often due to issues in early childhood, lack of education and lack of service availability to identify early onset. Within any assessment and treatment in psychiatry the primary tool is communication between the patient and professional. These communication issues not only affect face-to-face interviews but also the psychological tools used to guide diagnosis and treatment. These tools have never been validated on a Deaf population, and skewed results lead to Deaf people being misdiagnosed with 'learning disabilities' or with severe mental health problems going unnoticed and in some cases resulting in serious risks to themselves and others.

It is documented that Deaf people remain longer within acute inpatient services than their hearing peers due to lack of accessible services, poor community provision, or suitably qualified professionals to follow up their care (DoH, 2002). This all results in Deaf people receiving inadequate services which fail to meet all their needs. This sometimes becomes a double-edged sword, as professionals often have to prioritise mental healthcare needs over communication or vice versa. Community services which offer both communication and adequate mental health provision in a Deaf milieu are few and far between; they are often out of the person's local area and can become expensive for local authorities to fund.

With changes to patient directives, advances in connected health technology, digital communication aids and the trend in social media, access to appropriate communication support is easier and cheaper to obtain. This allows patients more choice in how they access services and requires less reliance on the support of others. The legal responsibility placed on services to improve accessibility should result in an improved access to services.

The following case studies are taken from an amalgamation of the lives of individuals both authors have met in practice. They illustrate issues common to Deaf people today. The cases illustrate the deep connection between Deaf people's lives, institutions, and policy and practice.

Case study 1

Josh was born in the 1980s to a mother who was unable to cope due to her own significant problems. Josh was adopted by a loving family who had two other children. As Josh developed it became evident that he was struggling to communicate despite being a bright child. At the age of two he was diagnosed as profoundly Deaf and there followed years of audiology support, hearing aid fitting, lip reading classes and parental support which enabled Josh to achieve well and to attend a good school for d/Deaf children.

The school used the Oral/Aural approach for all the pupils. The children also signed to each other outside class, so when Josh left school with three 'A' levels he had a good chance to get to university and to go on to get a decent job. Leaving the protection of his Deaf school, and teachers who understood his needs and peers with whom he shared his life experiences, was a huge step. Josh started a degree in Environmental Science at a small university in the Midlands. Despite initial assurances, the university staff found it challenging to provide the level of support Josh was used to at school. This unsettling time triggered feelings of anxiety and depression but this was missed for the first year at university until Josh refused to return after the summer break.

At the same time Josh began to look for his birth mother. This decision brought up overwhelming feelings for him and he found it difficult to express his emotions and was unable to explain to his family why he was so depressed.

His mother decided to take Josh to see his GP and acted as his communication support while at the appointment. Again, Josh was unable to express his feelings and his depression went undiagnosed. In the October of his second year at university Josh took an overdose of paracetamol. He was found and admitted to the local Accident and Emergency department, where health professionals assessed his mental health. At no point during the assessment did staff acknowledge Josh's lack of hearing by providing interpreters or other communication support mechanisms.

Josh went on to experience undiagnosed clinical depression for the next five years until he was eventually referred to the National Centre for Mental Health and Deafness.

Case study 2

Eve is 57 years old and has worked as a cleaner in the local council offices for over 40 years. She has worked in the same building with the same colleagues for over 10 years and until very recently has been very happy at work. Eve, a sign language user, was born into a Deaf family and is an active member of her local Deaf community. Eve is married to Tom, who is also Deaf and they have two hearing sons; both grown up with their own families and now living in different parts of the country. Eve has been caring for her husband, Tom, who is 10 years her senior and has recently been diagnosed with Alzheimer's dementia. His diagnosis had been problematic due to the couple being reluctant to seek help. His illness came to light following a recent fall and resulting fractured hip. Eve now needs support from home carers to help her get Tom up and ready in the morning and into bed at night.

Despite the language differences between the couple and with the people who come in to provide care, for the most part, Eve and the carers have been able to manage with some sign language, gestures and pen and paper. Unfortunately, due to reductions and changes to service provision, Eve and Tom are no longer visited by the same carers and have had to manage with different carers appearing each day and sometimes different carers within the same day. Eve is finding that the stress of working, caring and the changes in support are now impacting on her own physical and mental health. Eve cannot give up her job due to financial necessity; she is reluctant to allow Tom to go into a nursing home because there are no nursing homes suitable for Deaf people within travelling distance. Eve has taken all her annual leave for the year and has no more paid carer leave available.

Reflection

- What are the issues for Deaf people such as Josh, Eve and Tom accessing health care services?

- What are the communication issues and strategies that could be used to support Josh, Eve and Tom?

- What are the issues for education, and employment, for Deaf people? How are these linked to the individual's potential and society's perceptions of Deaf people?

Communication

In both case studies communication has broken down for all individuals at a familial, educational and healthcare level. This section will outline the pressures in regard to communication that d/Deaf people encounter. It is vital that we understand the difference between communication and language. Communication is the essential connection and information-giving process required for humans and other animals to understand their environment, those around them and their connections with their external and internal world. Communication can take a number of forms and utilise our senses: visual, auditory, gustatory, olfactory and tactile. We use visual and auditory channels for world languages, song, music, writing, pictures, gestures and visual language codes such as semaphore or Makaton. We use smells to communicate; for example, the 'baking bread' essence used in supermarkets, perfumes to suggest sensuality and coffee smells to help sell our houses to potential buyers. We use taste to communicate 'love'; some animals can taste the air to enhance their olfactory senses and access the information available in their environment. We communicate love, anger, fear, passion and trust through a variety of tactile sensations.

Focusing on the visual and auditory channels we can start to unravel d/Deaf and hard of hearing people's access to their world. Children born with limitations to their world through their auditory channel will require either auditory amplification if there is enough residual hearing for amplification to be useful. These children will also require specialist support in translating the auditory input into words and meaning. If the amplification route is not viable, children can develop their access by relying on their visual channel for the majority of their requirements. However, this does mean the translation of auditory input into visual input. This could be a flashing light to indicate someone is at the door, or a vibrating pad in the bed to wake the child.

The more complex issue, however, surrounds the language of the child, their family and their community. A profoundly Deaf child can learn the sign language of their community as easily as a hearing child can learn the spoken language. Visual languages and spoken languages are equally complex, equally functional and follow similar language rules. The Deaf child has a 5 per cent chance of having signing Deaf parents, which would be an ideal language environment; for the other 95 per cent of children about 10 per cent of their parents and siblings will learn sign language to include the Deaf child in their family as well as possible. The remaining majority of children will develop some signs, gestures and lip reading skills, often enough to get by at home but still not enough to have full access to family discussions, get-togethers and parties. Children who are excluded because of a lack of shared language are experiencing their first frustrations and limitations in life. Parents also face exclusion, as in the UK, 56 per cent of local authorities do not provide any means for parents to learn sign language when they have a signing child (NDCS, 2014).

Growing up in a limited language environment will affect the child's ability to understand their world and the relationships around them. This fundamental exclusion can have a powerful impact on the child's emotional and intellectual development and affect them throughout their lives. Positive options for an inclusive life require commitment from services in the form of speech and language therapists, audiologists, counsellors and Deaf role-models. Local authorities should provide well-supported pre-school and school access, including sign language classes for family members and educationalists who provide the most suitable access for the child. Unfortunately, for many children this utopian communication milieu does not exist or is limited in quality.

Communication strategies

Poor access to communication/information is often the main point of exclusion to education, health and social care for Deaf people. When education and health professionals are asked 'how you would communicate with a Deaf person?' they often report the following methods:

1. Use of pen and paper;

2. Lip reading thinking they have clear lip patterns;

3. Via a family member or friend who has accompanied them who signs;

4. They or a colleague may have some basic sign language skills; or

5. They have access to a BSL interpreter.

As outlined above, some Deaf people struggle in school, and so the use of written communication should only be relied upon if the professional knows that a) the deaf person is literate and b) how literate they are, because health discussions can be very detailed in nature requiring complex understanding of vocabulary and concepts. Signed language is not a direct translation from the English language as many people believe; it has its own grammatical structure and not all English words are translated. Metaphors are often lost in the translation of signed language.

Lip reading is not always an effective way to communicate, only 50–60 per cent of the conversation is understood by the very best readers of lips, it requires the speaker to have a good lip pattern, a regional accent similar to the Deaf person and that the Deaf person has knowledge of the words and lip pattern. So in health and education conversations where new meaning and new concepts are often required this can cause immense difficulty.

Deaf people, due to the exclusion they endure, will often arrive at appointments or meetings with family or friends who sign on their behalf. This raises issues for both the Deaf person and the professional in that neither truly knows if a correct translation has occurred. The Deaf person may not want to discuss personal issues in front of the family member and will therefore withhold vital information.

Sometimes non-signers think if a person can sign then that is good enough. Sign language, like any other language, has a range of fluency. Many people have studied 'signs for work' or BSL stage 1 and 2, but this would not give them the fluency required for a health or social care related conversation. Qualified interpreters are required in order to undertake such tasks.

The use of BSL Interpreters is a common strategy when working with Deaf people; the booking of interpreters is often easy when it is known who to call and the time is available to make the necessary arrangements. Booking interpreters becomes more complex in emergency situations or where there are time constraints. Rightly or wrongly, the issue of affordability and availability of funding to pay for interpreters often plays a part. The understanding of how to work with interpreters is equally important. Interpreters have specialist areas of work, e.g. education, health or law, and it is vitally important that interpreter is aware of the nature of the meeting, including the roles and responsibilities of those present. It is not as easy as *'just sign what I say'*, which is often asked of interpreters by people who do not understand their role or the culture and language issues the interpreter is managing.

It is important to understand that BSL interpreters are immersed within the Deaf community and may have social contacts with the Deaf person. In cases where the interpreter knows the Deaf person socially it would be inappropriate for them to interpret in certain types of meetings. With the emergence of new technology, interpreters and translators are available almost instantly via video media platforms, and it is vital that the people working with the interpreters understand how to use these new technologies.

Deaf people and employment

Given the multitude of issues that can face Deaf and hard of hearing people as they come into the world, grow up within their families, enter and leave their education with often (though not always) poorer results then their hearing counterparts, it should come as no surprise that Deaf and hard of hearing are more likely to be unemployed, underemployed and unrepresented in management, professional and skilled positions. Deaf women fare worse in the employment environment than Deaf men.

There are pockets of good practice where Deaf professionals have entered once inaccessible areas such as clinical and educational psychology, mental health nursing, nursery nursing, social work and teaching, but these examples are often of extremely dedicated and inspirational individual Deaf people, or projects specifically set up to widen access to certain professions (Sharples, 2013). They do not tend to be the result of a naturally occurring, positively accessible and inclusive profession.

Deaf children's education: the present context

We have reviewed the historical context of deaf education and need to bring the discussion up-to-date. Worldwide deaf education differs from country to country as does hearing children's education. For example, in some rural parts of sub-Saharan Africa deaf children cannot access the required technology nor the signing classes needed to attain in life. In other parts of the world the technology and desire for 'normalcy' is funded by the state, and deaf children are implanted as babies in an effort to minimise the excluding effects of deafness. These children then go on to mainstream schools to function as much as possible within the mainstream environment. In more accepting societies deaf children and parents are supported through state intervention to make the most of whichever communication channel and language mode provides the child with most access and therefore the most inclusion. Schools within these more open societies mirror the communication strategies and look to provide accessible education for children with a range of language and communication needs.

There are some wonderful examples of schools that take an oralist approach, others that take a signing stance and there remain some very poor examples too. What is evident is that the approaches taken to develop the child's communication environment and subsequently the child's education environment mirror each other and mirror each different society's response to deafness and disability and the economic health of the country and the country's education, and health institutions.

Conclusion

This chapter has taken an historical look at the experiences of Deaf people in Western societies. The two case studies illustrate the exclusion faced by Deaf people accessing health and social care services. The crucial factor is communication and the ability to access a communication milieu; this is the vital force that enables all other aspects of life to be fulfilled.

Despite a number of policies and legislation created to help Deaf people to prevent social exclusion, there has always been a misunderstanding of the Deaf community by a hearing non-deaf society regarding the real needs of Deaf people. We continue to focus our energy and funding on projects to restore hearing because Western society values normalcy. As we have seen throughout history, Deaf people and the inclusion or exclusion is not in their hands but in the hands of institutions and influential individuals. To be influential one needs to share common parlance with people in power and to do this one needs full and fair access to that language.

We have seen significant changes since 2003, not only with the recognition of BSL but also opportunities in new industries: for example, Deaf people now have access to Nursing Education, and there are 15 signing Deaf nurses on the professional nursing register. New technology allows Deaf people to access information and services never previously available to them. We are in no way saying that society has fully evolved to the inclusion of Deaf people, but the mind of society has started to shift towards the positive once more. The continuation of the positive shift relies heavily on non-Deaf people understanding the needs of this small minority and how decisions, policies, laws, systems and structures of institutions divest this responsibility equitably.

Recommended reading

- Davis, L.J. (2002) *Bending over Backwards: Disability, Dismodernism and other Difficult Positions*. New York: New York University Press.

- Groce, N.E. (1988) *Everyone Here Spoke Sign Language: Hereditary Deafness in Martha's Vineyard*. Cambridge: Harvard University Press.

- Ree, J. (1999) *I See a Voice. Deafness Language and the Senses*. New York: Henry Holt Publishing.

Relevant web links

- World Federation of the Deaf http://wfdeaf.org/

- Action on Hearing Loss www.actiononhearingloss.org.uk

- National Deaf Children's Society www.ndcs.org.uk

References

Adams, J.W. and Rohring, D.S. (2004) *Handbook to Service the Deaf and Hard of Hearing: A Bridge to Accessibility*. San Diego: Elsevier Academic Press.

Barnes, L. (2007) *Deaf Students in Higher Education: Current Research and Practice*. Coleford: Douglas McLean Publishing.

Branson, J. and Miller, D. (2002) *Damned for Their Difference: The Cultural Construction of Deaf People as Disabled*. Washington: Gallaudent University Press.

Davis, L.J. (1995) *Enforcing Normality: Deafness, Disability and the Body*. London: Verso.

_____(2002) *Bending over Backwards: Disability, Dismodernism and other Difficult Positions*. New York: New York University Press.

Department of Health (1997) *A Service on the Edge: Inspection Report of Social Services for Deaf and Hard of Hearing*. London: HMSO.

_____(1999) *Stepping Away from the Edge*. London: HMSO.

_____(2002) *A Sign of the Times*. London: HMSO.

_____(2005) *Towards Equity and Access*. London: HMSO.

_____(2011) *GP Patient Survey*. London: HMSO.

Disability Discrimination Act (1995) Elizabeth II. London: HMSO.

Equalities Act (2010) Elizabeth II. London: HMSO.

Giddens, A. (2006) *Sociology* (5th edn) Cambridge: Polity Press.

Groce, N.E. (1988) *Everyone Here Spoke Sign Language: Hereditary Deafness in Martha's Vineyard*. Cambridge: Harvard University Press.

Heslop, P. and Turnbull, S. (2013) Research into the Health of Deaf People. Ipsos Mori: London.

Hindley, P. and Kitson, N. (eds) (2000) *Mental Health and Deafness*. London: Whurr Publishers.

Kritzinger, J., Schneider, M., Swartz, L. and Braathen, S.H. (2014) I just answer 'yes' to everything they say: access to health care for Deaf people in Worcester, South Africa and politics of exclusion. *Patient Education and Counselling*, 94(3): 379–383.

Meadows-Orlands, K. and Erting, C. (2000) Deaf people in society. In P. Hindley and N. Kitson (eds) *Mental Health and Deafness*. London: Whurr Publishers.

National Deaf Children's Society (NDCS) (2014) *Access to BSL Learning for Families with Deaf Children in England*. London: Department of Education.

Obassi, C. (2007) Sign Language interpreting in higher education a period of progress? In L. Barnes, F. Harrington, J. Williams and M. Atherton (eds) *Deaf Students in Higher Education: Current Research and Practice*. Coleford: Douglas McLean Publishing.

Ree, J. (1999) *I See a Voice. Deafness Language and the Senses*. New York: Henry Holt Publishing.

Sharples, N. (2013) An exploration of Deaf women's access to mental health nurse education in the UK. *Nurse Education Today*, 33(9): 976–980.

8

DEMENTIA, DIVERSE COMMUNITIES AND ACCESS TO SERVICES

Anya Ahmed, Ubah Egal and Shahid Mohammed

Chapter overview: **key messages**

- Dementia – a progressive illness of the brain, most commonly affecting older people – has been identified as the biggest health and social care challenge facing society, due largely to an ageing population.
- Migration patterns from the 1950s and 1960s mean that the UK is now home to an ageing BME population, and there are currently 25,000 people with dementia from BME communities in England and Wales.
- This figure is expected to rise, yet little is known about the experiences of BME people with dementia, which in the UK includes people from a range of ethnic backgrounds.
- Although the National Dementia Strategy emphasises that health and social care service providers should take account of BME dementia needs, there is evidence that the needs of people from BME backgrounds are not currently being met.

Introduction

Dementia – a progressive illness of the brain, most commonly but not exclusively found in older people – has been identified as the biggest health and social care challenge facing society, due largely to an ageing population (All-Party Parliamentary Group on Dementia, 2013). At the 2011 Census, 16 per cent of the UK population were aged 65 and over, 14 per cent of whom were aged 85 and over, the population group that is growing fastest (ONS, 2013a). Migration patterns from the 1950 and 1960s mean that the UK is now home to an ageing Black and Minority Ethnic (BME) population (Ahmed, 2015a), and there are currently 25,000 people with dementia from BME communities in England and Wales (APPG, 2013). This figure is expected to rise to 50,000 by 2026 and 172,000 by 2051 (APPG, 2013). Yet little is known about the experiences of BME people with dementia, which in the UK includes people from a range of ethnic backgrounds. Although the National Dementia Strategy emphasises that health and social care staff should take account of BME dementia needs, service providers report challenges in including BME people (Williamson, 2012), and there is evidence that people from BME backgrounds are currently being 'failed' by the system (Moriarty et al., 2011). Additionally, among the UK's BME population there are lower levels of awareness of dementia and high levels of stigma associated with the condition. Further, people from BME backgrounds are underrepresented in dementia services and present to services later (Moriarty et al., 2011). However, there are no reliable figures and the evidence base is limited.

There is also a lack of research on BME communities and dementia. It has been suggested that there is a need to gather more information and engage with BME communities in order to fill gaps in knowledge about the particular service needs of BME people with dementia (Botsford and Harrison Dening, 2015) to successfully implement the National Dementia Strategy. Introduced in 2009 by the Department of Health, this strategy provides a framework within which local services can deliver quality improvements to dementia services and address health inequalities relating to dementia; provides advice and guidance and support for health and social care commissioners and providers in the planning, development and monitoring of services; and provides a guide to the content of services for dementia.

The chapter begins by clarifying our uses of the terms 'race', 'ethnicity' and 'culture'. We then outline the socio-demographic processes behind ageing and migration to establish the contextual background to the UK's older population. We provide a discussion of what dementia 'is' and the various forms that it can take, then outline the policy context, before presenting an overview of the issues facing BME communities with specific reference to the Dementia Care Pathway. We conclude by highlighting a number of measures which would need to be addressed to ensure the National Dementia Strategy's effective operation.

Reflection

What do you understand by the term dementia?

Understanding race, culture and ethnicity

The terms 'race', 'ethnicity' and 'culture' are often used interchangeably (Botsford, 2015). Race is usually used to refer to a group of people who share physical characteristics (Cartmill, 1998). However, it is now considered to be a controversial concept since it is based on Darwinian notions of biological and genetic difference between 'races' imbued with ideas of racial 'superiority' and 'inferiority'. The term 'race' privileges phenotypical, that is physical, traits and oversimplifies difference. As such, the concept of race is no longer currently considered to accurately depict difference and diversity; however, its use continues in everyday language in the terms 'racism' and 'race relations', for example (Botsford, 2015). Culture relates to people's 'way of life' or the way groups 'do things', with regard to values, behaviour, beliefs and attitudes, and particular cultures are often associated with different ethnic groups. Ethnic categories can be understood as forms of social organisation, with boundaries denoting who belongs (Anthias, 2002) and who does not. Ethnicity can be understood as being based on country of origin; it is also an identification and identifier, or a social position which has contextual meaning (Ahmed, 2015b). The terms 'Black and Minority Ethnic' (BME) and 'Black, Asian and Minority Ethnic' (BAME) are both commonly found in research and general literature. In this chapter we use the term 'Black and Minority Ethnic', abbreviated to BME, which also includes Asian and white minority ethnic groups. We also use the term 'minority ethnic' in preference to 'ethnic minority', since it captures the reality that everyone, regardless of nationality, belongs to an ethnic group.

Reflection

Why is using ethnicity a preferable term to race?

Socio-demographic processes behind ageing and migration in the UK

International migration has altered the age profile and ethnicity of the ageing population in the UK (Ahmed, 2015a) and migration, diversity and ageing are welfare policy priorities across Europe (White, 2007). During the 1950s and 1960s migrants from ex-British colonies arrived in the UK to fill gaps in the labour market in shipbuilding, metal manufacture, transport, textiles, foundry work and vehicle manufacture. At this time, these occupations were not attractive to the British workforce as they were poorly paid and involved long hours and shift work. Such migration was possible since at this time people from countries previously subjected to British imperial rule had unrestricted rights to a British passport (White, 2007). When migrants from the ex-colonies arrived in the UK it was during the period of high economic growth, and it was expected that they would eventually return 'home' when their labour was no longer needed; however, this did not happen. These 'Non-European Labour Migrants' (NELM) have 'aged in place' (Warnes et al., 2004) in the UK, and are one of the two categories of older migrants in Europe which are ageing the most rapidly (Warnes et al., 2004). As a result of previous migration, there is now a significant and diverse BME population in the UK which is reaching old age (White, 2007; Lievesley, 2010; Ahmed, 2015a).

On census day 2011, there were 1.25 million people aged 85 or over living in England and Wales, compared to 1.01 million in 2001 (ONS, 2013b). In 2011 13 per cent (7.5 million) of the resident population of England and Wales were born outside the UK compared to 4.3 per cent (1.9 million) in 1951, so migration has contributed to 45 per cent of the total population change over the last 60 years (ONS, 2013a). By 2051 it is estimated that the BME population in the UK will number 25 million people, which will comprise 36 per cent of the total. It is expected that the non-white population by 2051 will number 20 million people, or 29.7 per cent of the total population. Further estimates suggest that by 2051 there will be 3.8 million BME older people aged 65 and older, and 2.8 million aged 70 and older. In terms of the BME population, projections suggest that by 2051 there will be 2.7 million people aged 65 and over, and 1.9 million aged 70 and over (Lievesley, 2010). It is important to acknowledge that older BME populations are diverse both in terms of their country of origin and also regarding their levels of social capital (Warnes and Williams, 2006), which can impact on their knowledge of and use of services. Many of these migrants came from poor rural areas and had very limited education in their country of origin, and their subsequent poor economic situation in the UK often made them vulnerable to social exclusion (Torres, 2006).

Understanding dementia

Dementia is a growing global challenge. As the population ages, it has become one of the most important health and care issues facing the world. The number of people living with dementia worldwide today is estimated at 44 million people, set to almost double by 2030 (World Alzheimer's report 2014). In England, it is estimated that around 676,000 people have dementia (Dementia UK, 2014). As the population grows and ages, the economic burden of dementia is expected to rise significantly (Department of Health, 2013), and according to The King's Fund (2008), total annual spending on dementia is projected to reach £35 billion in 2026.

The term 'dementia' can be understood as an umbrella term to describe a set of brain diseases which cause gradual and long-term impairment to cognitive and physical functioning. The World Health Organization defines dementia as follows:

Dementia is a syndrome – usually of a chronic or progressive nature – in which there is deterioration in cognitive function (i.e. the ability to process thought) beyond what might be expected from normal ageing. It affects memory, thinking, orientation, comprehension, calculation, learning capacity, language, and judgement. Consciousness is not affected. The impairment in cognitive function is commonly accompanied, and occasionally preceded, by deterioration in emotional control, social behaviour, or motivation. (WHO, 2015)

Dementia is not part of 'normal ageing'; instead, there is a greater decline in thinking and physical functioning ability than is typically associated with ageing (Solomon and Budson, 2011). Dementia occurs when the brain is damaged by disease, such as Alzheimer's or caused by strokes, as is the case in vascular dementia. The most common type of dementia is Alzheimer's disease, with between 50 and 70 per cent of all cases of dementia falling into this category. Other common types of dementia include vascular dementia, which comprises approximately 20 per cent of all dementia cases. Other less known forms of dementia include Lewy bodies dementia (comprising approximately 15 per cent of all cases) and frontotemporal dementia (Solomon and Budson, 2011). It is not uncommon for people to have more than one form of dementia at the same time. The symptoms of dementia vary from person to person, and according to the type of dementia a person has (particularly in the early stages), since different parts of the brain are affected. However, the most common symptoms include memory and language loss, attention and problem-solving difficulties, as well as visual and spatial problems where people can experience hallucinations and are unable to navigate their physical environment. Additionally, people can experience and exhibit psychological and emotional difficulties. Dementia is a progressive condition, which means that the symptoms become more severe over time and currently there is no cure. The symptoms and progress of some types of dementia, for example Alzheimer's, can be treated by medication, and there is also some evidence that making lifestyle changes can delay the onset of vascular dementia.

People living with dementia (PWD) are usually deemed to be in one of three stages of the disease: early, middle or late. In the early stages of the disease, family members may notice changes in behaviour in terms of day-to-day memory and organisational skills. A person with early stage dementia may appear confused about where they are, be unable to follow a conversation or find the right word to describe something. As the disease progresses, in the middle stage, symptoms become more severe and changes in behaviour may occur, including agitation, restlessness and repetitive conversation patterns. During this stage, PWD may begin to withdraw socially. In the final stages of the disease, PWD often experience an inability to sleep and loss of appetite resulting in muscle wasting and significant weight loss. As the disease progresses, PWD and their caregivers need more support, and interventions from health and social care providers are important in fulfilling this role (Ahmed, Yates-Bolton and Collier, 2014).

Reflection

Why do you think that the early stages of dementia are difficult to identify?

The policy and practice context

The National Health Service is funded by Central Government through taxation and national insurance contributions (NIC). Social Service Departments (SSDs) are funded by grants from Central Government, again through taxation (Comas-Herrera et al., 2010). Since the NHS reforms in 2013, resources are distributed at regional level through Clinical Commissioning Groups (CCGs), which are responsible for commissioning health services, including dementia-related healthcare services as identified by Joint Strategic Needs Assessments (JSNA) of PWD. A range of public sector (NHS, social care services), private sector, voluntary sector and voluntary sector (charitable and BME specific) organisations provide a range of dementia-related care services, with provision ranging from pre-diagnosis to end of life care. All health and social care services are regulated by the Care Quality Commission.

The National Dementia Strategy (2009) and the Equality Act 2010 are the main legislative and policy frameworks addressing the issues relating to BME communities and dementia in the UK. In England and Wales, dementia care is mainly the responsibility of mental health providers rather than neurological services, as is the case in Scotland (Goodorally, 2015). The National Institute for Health and Care Excellence (NICE) has established a 'Dementia Care Pathway', which outlines how a PWD should experience services and how different services should connect. The Dementia Care Pathway can be summarised as having broadly six stages: First, **Prevention**, where awareness raising, risk reduction and the promotion of healthy living feature; second, **Identification**, where people would be referred to the Memory Service, usually following a GP appointment; third, **Assessment and Diagnosis**, when the Memory Service (or other specialist agency) carries out a full assessment. At this stage, if someone is given a diagnosis of dementia this would be explained. The fourth stage is **Early Intervention and Treatment:** from this stage, PWD are given an annual review and offered support and medication where appropriate. At this stage caregivers should also have their needs assessed and access to services should be explained. Fifth, **Living well with dementia**, PWD should have their needs regularly reviewed and appropriate interventions should be in place. Opportunities to plan for future care (and long-term care) should be provided alongside support and coping strategies for caregivers. The final stage of the pathway is **End of life care**; PWD should be added to the Palliative Care Register when they approach the end of their life and appropriate support should be in place. However, as we explain below, there is still a good deal of work to be done with and for PWD from BME communities at each stage of the Dementia Care Pathway.

Dementia and BME communities

As highlighted above, the numbers of people living with dementia from BME communities is set to rise exponentially, and the National Dementia Strategy (Department of Health, 2009) emphasises that health and social care services should take account of the needs of people from BME communities. However, service providers report challenges in meeting their needs (Williamson, 2012); there is a lack of representation of people from BME communities among health professionals and BME communities are underrepresented in dementia services (APPG, 2013). Evidence also suggests that there are lower levels of awareness about dementia among BME populations, and higher levels of stigma surrounding the disease (Moriarty et al., 2011). People from BME communities also present later to services (APPG, 2013). Although there are limited data currently available, it is likely that certain types of dementia, for example, vascular dementia, is more common among BME populations since some modifiable risk factors – hypertension, diabetes and high cholesterol – are more prevalent within such communities. For many communities, life expectancy in the UK may now significantly exceed life expectancy in their country of origin. This may mean a greater likelihood of them developing dementia than would be the case in the country they originate from.

Although there is a limited evidence base (Botsford and Harrison Dening, 2015), existing studies indicate that people from BME communities in the UK experience difficulties at each stage of the Dementia Pathway. For example, PWD from BME communities and their carers face barriers in accessing services and often access services at a later stage, when their dementia is more advanced. In many BME communities there is no word for 'dementia', which makes framing, describing and understanding the disease more difficult. There are also lower levels of awareness of dementia and often higher levels of stigma in some communities, which again can make identifying the disease and accessing services problematic. Lower levels of knowledge of dementia are also believed to contribute to higher levels of stigma: in some communities, dementia is associated with mental illness (Moriarty, 2015). Additionally, religion can influence people's perceptions of dementia and how they engage (or not) with support services (Moriarty, 2015). Religious beliefs can frame dementia as a punishment for behaviour in a past life (Hinton et al., 2008), a punishment from God (Adamson, 2001) or as possession or witchcraft (Jett, 2006). Services are often not culturally sensitive or appropriate, which can also create obstacles to access. Additionally, BME communities are stereotyped as 'looking after their own', which can mean that providers are reluctant to intervene (Moriarty et al., 2011). It is also important not to underplay the role of language: almost all minority ethnic people living in the UK aged 65 and over were born outside the UK, and even those who speak fluent English can gradually lose this ability as dementia progresses (Khan, 2015). Further, those people who are not fluent in speaking English are at a disadvantage when using health services (Botsford et al., 2012). For example, people may not be aware of available resources, or even if they access resources they may find it difficult to communicate with staff or to comprehend treatment options (Moriarty, 2015).

Reflection

Why are people from different ethnic groups less likely to seek support for dementia?

Therefore, low levels of awareness of dementia (and lack of knowledge of preventative measures), compounded by stigma surrounding the disease, pose challenges to PWD from BME communities in approaching healthcare services. General Practitioners essentially act as gatekeepers to accessing other primary care services and secondary care services and would be the first point of contact in the Dementia Care Pathway for someone who thought that they or a family member was showing symptoms of dementia. However, evidence suggests that GPs' awareness and understanding of dementia is not always robust, and this can result in a failure to diagnose and refer to other services. However, the Royal College of General Practitioners has raised questions about the value of early dementia diagnosis since post-diagnosis there are concerns about the levels of support that PWD and their carers receive from the NHS and social services (BBC July 2015).

For PWD from BME backgrounds, however, such difficulties in identifying dementia symptoms are compounded due to the additional challenges outlined above. Consider the case study below.

Case study

Jai is 19 years old, attends sixth-form college and hopes to go to university next year. Jai lives with both of his parents and younger sister, aged 15. Jai's father is disabled and Jai's mother is the caregiver. Recently, Jai has noticed that his mother has been 'under the weather' and very irritable, often becoming angry at relatively minor issues. At first, Jai put this down to tiredness due to her care-giving responsibilities, but some troubling instances have occurred, including forgetting to prepare meals and attend hospital appointments. Jai became extremely concerned on arriving home to find his sister locked out of the house and his father locked inside, and he was unable to locate his mother. His mother was later brought home by a neighbour who found her in a confused state in the local supermarket. Jai doesn't know what to do about the family's problems and he is unsure what steps to take next.

Reflection

- What would you do if this situation affected your family?
- Would you know which services to contact or which course of action to take?
- What do you think are the family's support needs?

If a person with suspected dementia is referred to the Memory Clinic for diagnosis, there are further challenges facing people from BME communities. Dementia is usually diagnosed by determining cognitive impairment and decline over time and by using screening instruments to measure the type and extent of cognitive impairment (Shah and Zarate Escudero, 2015). Originally, diagnostic screening tools were devised to test the majority ethnic group in the UK, and such tools are not appropriate for testing the cognitive function of PWD from BME backgrounds. There have been some developments in screening instruments for some BME groups (for example, the abbreviated Mental Test Score and the Mini Mental State Examination (MMSE)); however, these diagnostic tools can only be used by bilingual clinicians as the questions are in the original language of older BME community members. Further, there are no instruments which can be used by English-only speaking clinicians with an interpreter translating (Shah and Zarate Escudero, 2015). Clearly then, there are challenges at the assessment and diagnostic stages of the Dementia Care Pathway for PWD from BME communities. This in turn then has implications for early intervention, and delays in treatment, and can compromise a PWD's ability to live as well as is possible with dementia.

Reminiscence work is considered helpful for someone to live well with dementia; however, often, reminiscence therapies are not appropriate for people from a BME background, as British historical and cultural reference points are used (Ahmed et al., 2014).

Good practice example 1

BME Health and Wellbeing, a community organisation in Rochdale, produced a DVD on 'Purani Yaadein' (old memories) to raise awareness of dementia among the south Asian community in Rochdale and to capture the 'Purani Yaadein' of the first generation of south Asians who settled in the town.

The making of the film was inspired by the team's personal experiences (parents of the team members arrived in the UK in the 1960s to fill the labour shortage in the textile industry). The film captured a number of old memories of people from this early generation as part of the project, which also included community-based reminiscing workshops.

The film features interviews from healthcare professionals, including Dr Shanu Datta, Consultant Psychiatrist for Older People at Rochdale's Birch Hill Hospital, and Julie Mann, Dementia Adviser from the Alzheimer's Society.

Good practice example 2

The Somali dementia aware project

The Somali Cultural Centre in Kilburn (in partnership with the University of Salford) was funded by an Innovation Grant from Camden London Borough Council to conduct research on the experiences of the Somali community and dementia in the borough. The study aimed to fill gaps in knowledge about the Somali community's experiences of dementia; gather information about service needs and issues relating to access; gain an understanding of the levels of awareness of the needs of Somalis among service providers; and make recommendations for policy and practice and to raise awareness of dementia among Camden's Somali community.

It is only very recently (see Milne and Smith, 2015) that attention has been paid to the experiences and needs of PWD from BME backgrounds living in residential and nursing care homes. Take-up of care home services is low (Harrison Dening, 2015), possibly because of lack of knowledge of such services, issues with referrals and conflicts with religious and traditional patterns of care (Ahmed et. al., 2004; Koffman et al., 2007 and Werth et al., 2002, cited in Harrison Dening, 2015). Often, family members who are providing support do not identify as 'care-givers', so do not receive support themselves (Ahmed et al., 2014). Further, Western conventions and values shape decision-making processes in end of life care (Baker, 2002, cited in Harrison Dening, 2015). Additionally, social inequalities among older people can impact on end of life experiences since people's social and economic status during the course of their life is mirrored in the way that their death is perceived (Kinghorn, 2013). It is easier to exercise choices and control over end of life if a person is wealthy (Twomey et al., 2007) and again this could be an issue facing older BME communities in the UK (Ahmed, 2015a), particularly for PWD.

Conclusion

As a result of successive waves of migration, the UK is now a diverse and 'multicultural' society. However, different 'groups' in society experience different outcomes in relation to health, and it is widely acknowledged people from BME backgrounds have poorer general health outcomes than the majority ethnic population (Szczepura, 2005). This disparity is also evident in relation to outcomes regarding accessing dementia services, as we have explained. There is a historical legacy of not catering for the needs of BME older people, and a lack of knowledge about what their needs actually are (Ahmed, 2015a). Further, the intersection of old age and the migratory life course has important implications for older migrants' being at risk of marginalisation and social exclusion (Warnes et al., 2004; Torres, 2006; Ahmed, 2015a), and this can be further compounded for people living with dementia. There is a recognition among policy makers that older people with dementia from BME backgrounds face challenges in accessing healthcare, which makes them vulnerable and at risk of social exclusion (Shah and Zarate Escudero, 2015). However, it is important to acknowledge that many of the barriers affecting BME communities also affect the mainstream population: people do not always recognise the early symptoms and are unaware of where to go for help; they may be reluctant to approach their GP, or feel overwhelmed by the number of agencies that they need to engage with (Ahmed et al., 2014). Significantly too, austerity measures and cuts to welfare funding will pose new challenges to service providers (Ahmed, 2015a). Further, it is necessary to make the point that although it is inequitable not to address the dementia-related needs of older people from minority ethnic communities, it is problematic to overemphasise the differences from majority ethnic (or white) populations, since doing so can also lead to marginalisation (White, 2007; Ahmed, 2015a).

Throughout the course of this chapter we have established that people's ethnic and cultural backgrounds are significant in shaping their experiences of dementia and access to services. We presented a historical overview of migration to the UK and how older (NELM) migrants aged in place, and how this has subsequently led to a diverse and ageing population. We explained what dementia 'is' and provided a summary of the relevant policy context and have highlighted the issues facing BME communities with specific reference to the Dementia Care Pathway. We now conclude by presenting a series of recommendations which need to be addressed in order to successfully implement the National Dementia Strategy. First, there remains a need to engage with, and gather evidence in order to fill gaps in knowledge about, the service needs of people from different BME backgrounds (Botsford and Harrison Dening, 2015). Since BME communities are not homogenous, it is necessary to collect detailed and specific data (Ahmed et al., 2014). Second, information and publicity about dementia awareness and possible preventative measures needs to be disseminated among diverse communities through a range of culturally appropriate media (for example, community radio stations and posters), to dispel myths and remove the stigma surrounding dementia. Third, there needs to be transparency in processes to access relevant services at each stage of the pathway, from approaching GPs to making decisions about using care homes. Fourth, increased awareness of the needs of BME communities for gatekeepers (GPs) should be promoted. Fifth, there needs to be further development of culturally appropriate diagnostic screening tools, and culturally relevant reminiscence work. Sixth, there should be flexible and appurtenant support for carergivers.

Recommended reading

- All-Party Parliamentary Group on Dementia (2013) *Dementia Does Not Discriminate: The Experiences of Black, Asian and Minority Ethnic Communities*. London: APPG.

- Botsford, J. and Harrison Dening, K. (eds) (2015) *Dementia, Culture and Ethnicity: Issues for all*. London: Jessica Kingsley Publishers.

- Department of Health (2009) *Living Well with Dementia: A National Dementia Strategy*. Available at: www.gov.uk/government/uploads/system/uploads/attachment_data/file/168220/dh_094051.pdf.

- Moriarty, J., Sharif, N. and Robinson, J. (2011) *SCIE Research Briefing 35: Black and Minority Ethnic People with Dementia and Their Access to Support and Services*. London: Social Care Institute for Excellence.

Relevant web links

- www.alzheimers.org.uk
- www.dementiaaction.org.uk

- www.dementiafriends.org.uk
- www.scie.org.uk/publications/briefings/files/briefing35.pdf

References

Adamson, J. (2001) Awareness and understanding of dementia in African/Caribbean and South Asian families. *Health and Social Care in the Community,* 9: 391–396.

Ahmed, A., Yates-Bolton, N. and Collier, E. (2014) *Diversity and Inclusiveness in Dementia: Listening Event Report,* Salford: University of Salford.

Ahmed, A. (2015a) UK migration and welfare regimes. In U. Karl and S. Torres (eds) *Ageing in the Context of Migration.* London: Sage.

_____(2015b) *Retiring to Spain: Women's Narratives of Nostalgia, Community and Belonging.* Bristol: Policy Press.

All-Party Parliamentary Group on Dementia (2013) *Dementia Does Not Discriminate: The Experiences of Black, Asian and Minority Ethnic Communities.* London: APPG.

Alzheimer's Society (2016) *What Is Dementia?* Available at: www.alzheimers.org.uk/site/scripts/documents.php?categoryID=200360 (accessed 23 November 2015).

Anthias, F. (2002) Where do I belong?: Narrating identity and translocational positionality, *Ethnicities,* 2(4): 491–515.

Botsford, J., Clarke, C.L. and Gibb, C.E. (2012) Dementia and relationships: experiences of partners in minority ethnic communities. *Journal of Advanced Nursing,* 68: 2207–2217.

Botsford, J. and Harrison Dening, K. (2015) *Dementia, Culture and Ethnicity: Issues For All.* London: Jessica Kingsley Publishing.

Cartmill, M. (1998) The status of the race concept in physical anthropology. *American Anthropologist Association,* 100(3): 651–660.

Comas-Herrera, A., Pickard, L., Wittenberg, R., Malley, J. and King, D. (2010) *The Long-term Care System for the Elderly in England* (ENEPRI Research Report No. 74).

Department of Health (2009) *Living Well with Dementia: A National Dementia Strategy.* London: Department of Health.

_____(2010) *Quality Outcomes for People with Dementia: Building on the Work of the National Dementia Strategy.* London: Department of Health.

_____(2013) *Dementia: State of the Nation.* London: Department of Health.

Goodorally, V. (2015) Access, assessment and engagement. In J. Botsford and K. Harrison Dening (eds) *Dementia, Culture and Ethnicity: Issues for All.* London: Jessica Kingsley Publishing.

Harrison Dening, K. (2015) End of life, dementia and black and minority ethnic groups. In J. Botsford and K. Harrison Dening (eds) *Dementia, Culture and Ethnicity: Issues For All.* London: Jessica Kingsley Publishing.

Hinton, L., Nhauyen Tran, J., Tran, C. and Hinton, D. (2008) Religious and spiritual dimensions of the Vietnamese dementia caregiving experience. *Hallym International Journal of Ageing,* 10: 139–160.

Jett, K.F. (2006) Mind-loss in the African American community: dementia as a normal part of ageing. *Journal of Aging Studies,* 20: 1–10.

Khan, O. (2015) Dementia and ethnic diversity. In J. Botsford and K. Harrison Dening (eds) *Dementia, Culture and Ethnicity: Issues for All*. London: Jessica Kingsley Publishing.

Kinghorn, K. (2013) Death and the end of life. In P. Dwyer and S. Shaw (eds) *An Introduction to Social Policy* (pp. 113–127). London: Sage.

Lievesley, N. (2010) *Older BME People and Financial Inclusion Report: The Future Ageing of the Ethnic Minority Population of England and Wales*. London: Runnymede.

Milne, A. and Smith, J. (2015) Dementia, ethnicity and care homes. In J. Botsford and K. Harrison Dening (eds) *Dementia, Culture and Ethnicity: Issues For All*. London: Jessica Kingsley Publishing.

Moriarty, J., Sharif, N. and Robinson, J. (2011) *SCIE Research Briefing 35: Black and minority ethnic people with dementia and their access to support and services*. London: Social Care Institute for Excellence.

Moriarty, J. (2015) Accessing support and services. In J. Botsford and K. Harrison Dening (eds) *Dementia, Culture and Ethnicity: Issues for All*. London: Jessica Kingsley Publishing.

Office for National Statistics (2013a) *What Does the 2011 Census Tell Us About Older People?* Available at: www.ons.gov.uk/ons/rel/census/2011-census-analysis/what-does-the-2011-census-tell-us-about-older-people-/index.html (accessed 6 February 2016).

_____(2013b) *What Does the 2011 Census Tell Us About the "Oldest Old" Living in England & Wales?* Available at: www.ons.gov.uk/ons/rel/mortality-ageing/characteristics-of-older-people/what-does-the-2011-census-tell-us-about-the-oldest-old-living-in-england-and-wales-/characteristics-of-the--oldest-old--from-the-2011-census.html (accessed 7 February 2016).

Shah, A. and Zarate Escudero, S. (2015) Dementia and ethnicity. In J. Botsford and K. Harrison Dening (eds) *Dementia, Culture and Ethnicity: Issues For All*. London: Jessica Kingsley Publishing.

Solomon, A, and Budson, P. (2011) *Memory Loss: A Practical Guide for Clinicians*. Edinburgh: Elsevier Saunders.

Szczepura, A. (2005) Access to health care for ethnic minority populations. *Postgraduate Medical Journal,* 81: 141–147.

Torres, S. (2006). Culture, migration, inequality and "periphery" in a globalized world: Challenges for ethno- and anthropogerontology. In J. Baars, D. Dannefer, C. Phillipson and A. Walker (eds) *Ageing, Globalization and Inequality: The New Critical Gerontology* (pp. 231–251). Amityville, NY: Baywood Publishing.

_____(2012). International migration: patterns and implications for exclusion in old age. In T. Scharf and N. C. Keating (eds), *From Exclusion to Inclusion in Old Age: A Global Challenge* (pp. 33–50). Bristol: Policy Press.

Twomey, F., McDowell, D. and Corcoran, G. D. (2007) End-of-life care for older patients dying in an acute general hospital: can we do better? *Age and Ageing,* 36: 462–464.

Warnes, A.M., Friedrich, K., Kellaher, L. and Torres, S. (2004) The diversity and welfare of older migrants in Europe. *Ageing and Society,* 24: 307–326.

Warnes, A.M. and Williams, A. (2006) Older migrants in Europe: a new focus for migration studies. *Journal of Ethnic and Migration Studies,* 32: 1257–1281.

White, P. (2007) Migrant populations approaching old age: prospects in Europe. *Journal of Ethnic and Migration Studies.* 32: 1283–1300.

Williamson, T. (2012) *A Stronger Collective Voice for People with Dementia*. London: JRF.

World Health Organization (2015) Dementia Fact sheet No 362. Available at: www.who.int/mediacentre/factsheets/fs362/en/ (accessed 7 February 2016).

9

OLDER WOMEN'S EXPERIENCES OF DOMESTIC VIOLENCE AND ABUSE

Michaela Rogers

Chapter overview: **key messages**

- The term 'domestic violence and abuse' (DVA) refers to the gender-based nature of violence and abuse in intimate and family relationships (as opposed to the gender-neutral term 'elder abuse').
- Older women belong to a hidden group of victims/survivors of DVA.
- There are general barriers to help-seeking behaviour for people experiencing DVA as well as more specific ones pertaining to this age group.
- A multi-agency response is critical to helping older women leave abusive relationships and move towards recovery with appropriate support.

Introduction

Domestic violence and abuse (DVA) is a global problem and developing appropriate responses is a challenge for health and social care services (Lombard and McMillan, 2013). Not only is DVA entrenched and wide-reaching, it assumes many forms and has lasting impacts. There is no singular type of 'perpetrator', nor a homogenous group of 'victims' or 'survivors'. DVA affects people of all ethnicities, cultures, religious communities, sexual orientations, genders, socio-economic classes, geographies, mental capacities and physical abilities at any point during the life-course. However, it has been highlighted that the neglect of older women in DVA research and practice 'has been a silent and unconscious one [as d]omestic violence institutions as well research on domestic violence often maintain a focus upon young and middle aged women' (Goergen, 2011: 1). Inasmuch, older women constitute a 'hidden group' of victims/survivors (Turner et al., 2010). Indeed, in the UK one of the major surveys which is relied upon to collect statistical data on DVA does not include people aged 60 and over.

When abuse is identified, often it is problematically labelled as 'elder abuse' (Hightower, 2002). This does not recognise the distinct and gendered dynamics of power and control that often characterise DVA and while it is acknowledged that men can be victims too, more women experience DVA. Therefore, this chapter is concerned with the experiences of older women who, like younger women, experience DVA in considerable numbers and who experience physical, sexual, emotional and psychological harm as a result. There are, however, dynamics and impacts that are specific to this group of women as well as a complex number of barriers to making disclosures and seeking formal help. In light of this discussion, the chapter ends by outlining some messages for health and social care practice.

Domestic abuse and an ageing population

Despite women making up most of the older population in virtually all of the world's nations, the needs of older women who experience DVA have been given scant attention (Zink et al., 2004). There are, however, significant implications for research, practice and policy as global demographic trends, in terms of the ageing population, are 'unprecedented', 'pervasive' and 'enduring' (UN, 2002). Indeed, within the UK it is estimated that by 2030 there will be 51 per cent more people aged 65 or over compared to 2010 figures, and 101 per cent more people aged 85 or over (HM Government, 2013). This seemingly unstoppable trend will have considerable economic, political, cultural and social implications (HM Government, 2013) and present current and future challenges which will require state prioritisation, planning and funding. Such implications are currently unnamed, or hidden within the older population as these issues are yet to receive the attention they warrant; DVA being a prime example.

Elder abuse or domestic violence?

The 'naming' of abusive behaviour as one thing or another is important, particularly in this context where the discussion relates to a hidden and invisible group of victims/survivors (Turner et al., 2010). This invisibility makes the task of labelling pertinent, as the danger is that by misnaming the phenomenon – in addition to ignoring the subjective experience of the community (of older women) – the issue of older women and DVA becomes marginal, and of little consequence.

Throughout this chapter the Home Office term 'domestic violence and abuse' (DVA) refers to:

any incident or pattern of incidents of controlling, coercive, threatening behaviour, violence or abuse between those aged 16 or over who are, or have been, intimate partners or family members regardless of gender or sexuality. The abuse can encompass, but is not limited to: psychological; physical; sexual; financial; emotional. (Home Office, 2013: online)

It is useful to compare this to an understanding of elder abuse. In 1993 the UK charity, Action on Elder Abuse, proffered the following definition of elder abuse as:

a single or repeated act or lack of appropriate action, occurring within any relationship where there is an expectation of trust, which causes harm or distress to an older person .... [There are] five common types of abuse: physical, psychological, financial, sexual abuse and neglect. (Action on Elder Abuse, 2015: online).

At its core, this definition has the 'expectation of trust' which an older person may establish with another person, but which is then violated. Thus, the delineation of elder abuse excludes strangers. This definition has subsequently been adopted by the World Health Organization as well as many countries throughout the world. While there are other definitions of both DVA and elder abuse to be found, the ones included here are representative of most of these. More importantly, comparing these definitions, it is easy to find similarities; abuse is constituted by an incident or as a pattern of behaviour; abuse and violations are perpetrated by a person known to the victim; and the behaviour causes harm.

There is an important difference, however. In the majority of cases of DVA, the aim is to exert power of control over an individual; this is not necessarily the case in elder abuse. Yet some authors argue that DVA is a subset of elder abuse (Turner et al., 2010), while others critique this approach, arguing that it reproduces a structural predisposition to homogenise older populations by neglecting individual differences (Beaulaurier et al., 2008). The latter is an example of ageism, as neglect particularity in terms of older people's life experiences reflects a general decline in the respect and value placed on older people in societies throughout the world (WHO/INPEA, 2002). In addition, as noted by Lombard and Scott (2013), in cases of abuse, sexism intersects with ageism and so the construction of elder abuse is unhelpful, as it masks the power and dynamics which characterise DVA, as well as glossing over the notion that DVA is a gender-based crime that women experience disproportionately. In trying to account for the tendency to name DVA as elder abuse, it is evident that the social construction of old age – with connotations of frailty, vulnerability and general decline – has influence. Exploring this narrative of deficit in old age, Hightower (2002: 1) notes how the term 'elder abuse' is problematic as it reflects 'a view of the elderly as sexless, in which male and female victims of elder abuse are indistinguishable'. Moreover, Kelly and Johnson (2008) propose that in cases of DVA it is not the age of the victim/survivor that intensifies the individual experience, rather that the impact of DVA is compounded by ageism.

For all intents and purposes then, the position taken in this chapter is one in which the Home Office definition of DVA is employed to explore the experiences of older women who experience gender-based abuse as part of an intimate or familial relationship where there are elements of power and control. This approach also recognises gender inequality at a structural and institutional level; an important proposition that explains the ingrained and enduring nature of DVA in modern societies (Stark, 2007). Older women may be harmed by spouses or partners in heterosexual or lesbian relationships, by older/adult children or other family members or carers. Often, the types of abuse (physical, sexual, psychological, emotional and material) are experienced in combination, rather than as discrete incidents.

Finally, it is worth noting that there is a proliferation of terms used to name DVA (domestic violence, domestic abuse, intimate partner abuse, gender-based violence to name a few). It is important to note, however, that in terms of contemporary understandings, the work of Evan Stark (2007) has reconceptualised DVA as 'coercive control'. The concept of coercive control, while recognising the considerable effects of physical violence, emphasises the psychological and emotional impacts of the ways in which men oppress, control and entrap women in personal life and through everyday controlling behaviour. Stark's analysis moves from the micro to the macro to consider the daily abuse experienced by women by locating this within the societal problem of gender inequality. In this way, Stark argues that the abuse of women is a human rights violation as it limits a women's autonomy and freedoms and serves to sustain and reinforce gender inequality. The concept of coercive control has now been incorporated into the legal framework that addresses DVA (see below).

Challenges in measuring prevalence and analysing experience

Despite the acknowledged problems with collating prevalence data on DVA in the UK (for example, resulting from under-reporting); figures do tend to illustrate its gendered nature. Statistics consistently show that one in four women will experience DVA during their lifetime (as opposed to one in six men) and that two women are killed each week by their current or former partner (Guy et al., 2014). However, one of the problems in measuring prevalence in older women is that the Crime Survey for England and Wales (formerly the British Crime Survey) only collects data from people aged 16 to 59 (ONS, 2015a). So, for the period 2013/2014, statistics collected in the survey suggest that for people aged 16 to 59, 28.3 per cent of women (c. 4.6 million female victims) and 14.7 per cent of men (c. 2.4 million male victims) had experienced some form of DVA since the age of 16 (ONS, 2015b). In addition, women were more likely than men to have experienced DVA whatever the type (physical, sexual, psychological and financial) (ONS, 2015b). In addition, the current literature offers some insight into the scope and nature of DVA for younger populations (McGarry et al., 2011). As a consequence, it has been argued that statistics and contemporary literature on DVA lend themselves to a particular discourse, often where DVA is the embodiment of heterosexual masculinity which is then enacted against younger and child-bearing female bodies (Blood, 2004; Donovan and Hester, 2014). Put another way, DVA is predominantly a problem of the younger generations, where men are the perpetrators and women are the victims.

As such, older women constitute a population whose victimhood is 'hidden', as they are seldom included in DVA research, nor do they regularly access domestic abuse interventions (Blood, 2004; Women's Aid, 2007; McGarry et al., 2011). Consequently, there is no firm data about the extent of DVA perpetrated against women in later life. In addition, it is difficult to qualify what is meant by 'older women' or 'women in later life', as definitions of 'older' are usually based on chronological age only and existing research variously defines 'older' as starting at 40, 45, 50 and older (Scott et al., 2004; Lombard and Scott, 2013). This raises questions about the problem of homogenising experience, or of comparing the experience of a 45 year old woman to that of a 70 year old woman. This is why it is critical to differentiate between the ages of older women (Weeks and LeBlanc, 2011). It may be more useful to think about life stages and the shared social experiences that women may have (Lombard and Scott, 2013). This approach helps to move away from a chronological perspective and can give indicators in terms of capabilities, supports and needs in relation to life course stages (for example, mid-life being 40 to 55 and early later-life lasting from 55 to 70 (55 being the earliest age to retire), then 70 plus being later-life).

Reflection

How common do you think DVA is in older age groups? Do you think there is any difference in terms of the life stage periods identified above?

This section has demonstrated some of the difficulties of gaining a picture of the prevalence of DVA as experienced by older women. However, some statistical data is available and gives some indication of the extent of the problem. For example, a study by O'Keefe et al. (2007) found that more than 250,000 older people (aged 66 and older) living in England in private households reported experiencing maltreatment from a family member, close friend or care worker in the past year. Additionally, 31 per cent of respondents experienced abuse from a partner, 49 per cent from another family member, 5 per cent from a close friend and 13 per cent from a care worker. Women were more likely to experience maltreatment than men, and men were more often the perpetrators (O'Keefe et al., 2007).

Dynamics of abuse in later life

To form an appropriate response to cases of DVA, it is important to understand the dynamics in operation. For example, an older woman may find herself single due to the death of a spouse or through divorce, and she may enter a new relationship with a partner who is abusive. This relationship might have very different dynamics and impacts to a marriage which has lasted forty years. However, in both cases the emotional ties (feelings of guilt, shame, duty and loyalty) are very problematic and this may result in a victim living with abuse for some time before seeking help. For women who experience inter-generational abuse (abuse perpetrated by adult children or grandchildren), there are additional factors which create extra complexities. Victims/survivors may feel that they wish to protect their child or grandchild, rather than focusing upon their own safety and well-being. In these cases, the naming of abuse is obscured by the interplay of the relational bond along with feelings of embarrassment, failure, responsibility and love. Abusers can draw from many forms of abuse (physical, sexual, emotional, psychology and financial) along with some age-related abuses, particularly if the older grand/parent has physical or cognitive impairments. For instance, constant threats to place someone in a nursing home can have a powerful emotional and psychological effect in combination with the impacts of neglect, physical violence and financial abuses.

For older women who are ill or who have a disability, the abuser may also be their carer, or the abused woman may be the carer for a partner or adult child who is the perpetrator of DVA. In fact, illness and/or disability can provide the means by which to perpetrate abuse: for example, by withholding medicines or mobility aids, or controlling access to medical services and appointments. In previous years, caregiver stress (the considerable stress experienced by some-one who cares for another) has been mooted as a cause of DVA in later life, but current research does not support this claim (Wolf, 2000; Turner et al., 2010). For older women, ill health or disability may even be the results of earlier abuse (LGA, 2015). Disability, ill health or mobility problems can be given as the reasons why victims have bruises and injuries. Here practitioners can fail to recognise injuries resulting from DVA if they are more ready to accept the explanation given for an injury as being due to falls or an age-related condition (Women's Aid, 2007). Where dementia is present, it may be used to psychologically control and manipulate, or used to justify certain behaviours and actions. For example, an abuser who insists on never leaving the side of a woman who has been recently diagnosed with dementia can justify his/her behaviour as one of the loving, attentive partner (rather than a controlling abuser who monitors and controls the movement, time and actions of their victim). If a perpetrator has dementia, another medical condition or a mental health problem which affects behaviour, women can experience maltreatment and harm. In these cases some of the generic interventions offered by DVA services, such as safety planning and legal advocacy, can be helpful.

In addition, an older woman who is ill or has a disability may not have as many options or resources as a younger, healthier woman (Brandl and Dawson, 2011). So, for an older woman who experiences illness and DVA, there are multiple dimensions of marginalisation. There are, however, many older women who are healthy and active, but there can be additional factors which are associated with this stage in the life course. Lombard and Scott (2013: 127) point out some of these as being 'women who are no longer of childbearing age, or women who have stopped work and can draw their "old age" pension'. The first evokes the notion of 'transition' as a period of the life course which brings about significant changes to identity, role and status within the context of an intimate relationship or family network (in addition to more practical and economic changes). Indeed, identity abuse (abuse directed at some aspect of an individual's identity, or difference) is a powerful form of DVA that can serve to isolate, humiliate and exploit. The second point presents the financial status of older women as an opportunity to exert control and as a means of creating dependency, especially for those who have no formal education, employment record outside of the home, and who may lack economic resources independent of the abuser (LGA, 2015).

Reflection

What might be some of the effects of DVA for older women?

Think about social, cultural, physical, emotional and economic impacts.

You might consider loss of family and friends relationships, loss of community, rejection by family or communities, impact on parent/child relationship, lack of independence, social isolation, restricted/no access to community/church, loss of confidence and self-esteem, depression, anxiety, suicidal ideation/suicide, short-term and lasting injury or even death, broken bones, sensory loss (hearing or sight impairment), brain trauma, gastric problems, memory loss or sight impairment, low immune system, alcohol or other substance misuse problems, loss of income, loss of employment, loss of home and property.

Barriers to help-seeking action

The discussion so far has begun to explore some of the reasons why older women do not leave abusive relationships. These reasons are complex and multiple with barriers to recognising and identifying maltreatment, as well as to reporting and making contact with support agencies. A study by the National Centre for Social Research in 2007 found that there were various personal circumstances of an older person which prevented them from seeking help, including low self-confidence and self-esteem, experience of bereavement, physical frailty, perception of the seriousness, of the abuse and concerns about the consequences of taking action (Mowlam et al., 2007). This last point has multiple potential consequences including:

- fear of isolation;
- fear of being seen to be 'making a fuss';
- fear of being blamed;
- embarrassment;
- concerns for the well-being of the victim's family and significant others;
- concerns for the health and well-being of the perpetrator;
- fear of the abuse becoming worse. (Mowlam et al., 2007: 34)

There can also be worries about economic difficulties or losses that may be incurred: the prospect of living in poverty or leaving an established home can be very difficult. There may be concerns of ending up in residential care and losing independence (Brandl and Dawson, 2011). In cases where an adult child is the abuser, there may be issues about making the perpetrator homeless or worries about how they will manage, financially or otherwise, without their mother to take care of them. In addition, mothers can continue to feel responsibility for the actions of a child, however old they may be.

Many of the behaviours employed in cases of DVA in later life reflect those of younger women and a power and control dynamic is common (Brandl and Dawson, 2011). Indeed, older women may similarly fear the repercussions if they leave or attempt to end a relationship; in these instances this can include serious injury or homicide (Brandl et al., 2007; Beaulaurier et al., 2008). Decision-making, overall, can be troublesome and worrying as older women feel unable to make decisions for themselves and in isolation. Victims/survivors may feel that they are unable to make active choices as support services do not exist for older women; the perception being that DVA or safeguarding services are available to younger women or those with children. It is these types of assumptions that prevent women from leaving abusive relationships.

As noted previously, there are significant differences too in terms of the experience of older women compared with those of younger women. This is particularly so if abuse has been perpetrated over a period of time, as dependency (including financial dependency) may be deep-rooted and complicated by the traditional and religious values and attitudes held about marriage and gender roles (LGA, 2015). While these are intrapersonal and psychological concerns, there are also external barriers in terms of the lack of specific support for older victims. This has been highlighted in several reports and attributed to the problem that health and social care professionals fail to recognise DVA as occurring in this age group (Women's Aid, 2007; McGarry et al., 2011). When older women present with the symptoms of an abusive relationship (for example, depression, anxiety or even injuries) these can be put down to age and frailty. When abuse is recognised as elder abuse this may be due to the assumptions and social norms held that are associated with elder abuse (and ultimately the failure to acknowledge the gendered power dynamics inherent in abusive relationships in later life). Again, this may reflect the tendency to view DVA as a problem of younger generations.

Case study: **Rita**

Two years previously, 59 year old Rita and her husband, Jim, had moved from Ireland to be nearer to their eldest daughter, Clare, in a semi-rural community in the north of England. Jim had been physically and sexually abusive throughout their forty-year marriage. He was also a controlling and manipulative man who did not let Rita have an equal say or any independence. Rita came from a strict Catholic background; she did not believe in divorce and stayed with Jim until his death one year earlier. While Rita was financially secure, she had never made a decision about finances or bills, nor had she ever been in paid employment. Rita started a new relationship with Colin and agreed for his daughter and her partner, Wayne, to move in while they saved for the deposit on a house. Colin lived in an apartment and did not have the space, but Rita lived in a three bedroom semi-detached house and could afford to help Colin and his family. Just when she thought that her mother was moving on from her bereavement, Clare noticed a change in Rita, who appeared to be anxious, low in mood, and on one occasion Clare saw bruises on her mother's arm (Rita told Clare that she wasn't sure how she had got them). Rita did, however, confide to Clare that she thought that Wayne had taken some money from her purse and a couple of ornaments had gone missing.

Reflection

Consider the dynamics of this situation. What might be the challenges for Rita in terms of seeking some formal help from agencies? What might help facilitate her to obtain help and take action?

This case study clearly shows complex dynamics. Rita might be experiencing unresolved trauma from the long-standing DVA that she experienced during her marriage to Jim. This could be considered to be post-traumatic stress. She may lack the psychological and emotional strength needed to deal with the current situation. She may feel that she is responsible for what is occurring. There may be an additional pressure because of her relationship with Colin and the responsibility she feels for looking out for his daughter. Rita may be concerned that Colin will not believe her, or that he would blame her for what is happening. Rita may be worried about being on her own again. Generational, traditional and religious values and attitudes may influence Rita's feelings of duty, resignation to what is happening, and resistance to contacting agencies for support and advice. Rita may not want to 'rock the boat' or upset anyone by 'making trouble' or by causing 'a fuss'. These are all barriers to help-seeking. There may not be any services in Rita's immediate community; she may not know there are formal agencies that help victims of DVA. She may think those that exist are for 'young folk'. Rita might worry about other people knowing her business, particularly if speaking out meant that agencies, including uniformed police officers, would be visiting her home.

Enablers for help-seeking

In their study of the abuse and neglect of older people Mowlam et al. (2007) were able to identify two key facilitators that enabled older women to take action for change. These were fear for personal safety, and encouragement and support from others. Participants indicated that fearing for their personal safety could lead to action to source formal support and help to stop the abuse. One participant described how she had experienced DVA for many years before her partner crossed 'a red line' and this triggered help-seeking. Contained within this short vignette there is an important lesson for practitioners. For some women, the point at which they seek help might be the critical incident in which health and social care workers are enabled to support someone to make the difficult transition to leave an abuser. Not providing the right combination and appropriate level of support at this time can act as a barrier to the victim in successfully leaving. A victim may become resigned to living with abuse.

The second point raised by Mowlam et al. (2007) relates to the first, as their study found that victims are best supported to move on from abuse, and become survivors, when they have encouragement from others. This may be from informal sources (family members and friends) and more formal support (such as social workers, police, GPs and care workers). Reassurance, moral support, advocacy and advice from these sources are critical facilitators to moving forward from a life of abuse. In how to approach this type of work, Tuner et al. (2010) advocate taking the time necessary to build rapport and a relationship with women who are victims of DVA in later life.

DVA and the legal framework

In seeking to understand older victim's experiences, it is useful to contextualise this within the ever-changing, hotchpotch of law that governs the criminal justice sector's response to DVA. Currently, there is no singular act that legislates for 'domestic violence' as an offence in criminal law. Aspects of physical abuse, sexual assault, harassment and stalking, for example, are legislated for as unlawful within different acts. However, the lack of a specific offence persists despite the fact that the Ministry of Justice (MoJ) created a statutory definition of 'domestic violence' as 'any incident of threatening behaviour violence or abuse (whether psychological, physical, sexual, financial or emotional) between individuals who are associated with each other' (Legal Aid, Sentencing and Punishing of Offenders Act, 2012). This definition was constructed in response to the need for criteria for Legal Aid, rather than to influence a transformation in the legal framework underpinning criminal responsibility and DVA. As Groves and Thomas (2014: 17) note, 'statutory definitions are not indicative of what behaviour constitutes "an offence", rather; they acknowledge and define a range of behaviours as criminal "in nature"'. This means that while the MoJ (2012) and Home Office (2013) definitions discussed above are useful, neither have been directly influential in terms of current forms of legal redress for victims, as the specific types of DVA contained within the definition (physical, psychological, emotional, sexual and financial abuse) are not legislated for as offences as individual types of DVA.

Groves and Thomas (2014) argue that the most significant singular act in terms of indicating the Government's commitment to tackling DVA is the Domestic Violence, Crime and Victim Act 2004. An amendment in 2012 strengthened the Act, which essentially serves to provide the infrastructure support and protection for victims/survivors. It includes various forms of legal redress and incorporates the power of arrest for perpetrators who break protective orders such as a non-molestation order. Non-molestation orders require the 'molestation' to cease. In this sense, molestation includes acts of violence, threats, intimidation and harassment. Non-molestation orders are legislated for within the Family Law Act 1996 Part IV, which includes additional provisions to protect victims/survivors, such as occupation orders (which may give a victim a right to live in a property and exclude the perpetrator).

Over the years there have been various additions and updates, but a significant legal change has taken place more recently, as in 2015 the UK Government embedded an understanding of Stark's (2007) concept of coercive control within legislation. The offence of controlling or coercive behaviour in intimate or familial relationships (section 76) was created in the Serious Crime Act 2015, which received royal assent in March 2015. The offence attempts to 'close the gap' in terms of the current legal framework of relevant criminal offences (Home Office, 2015). It means that perpetrators can now be prosecuted for 'controlling or coercive behaviour' which is enacted 'repeatedly or continuously'; it is considered to be 'a purposeful pattern of behaviour' which has a 'serious effect' (Home Office, 2015: 3–4). As this is a new piece of legislation, its impacts are currently unknown. It does, however, add to the complex mix of laws in operation.

Reflection

Think of some types of behaviour which might fit the definition of 'controlling and coercive behaviour'.

Try to imagine the impacts of living with these types of behaviour. Consider an older woman who has recently been bereaved and started a new relationship that becomes abusive. Also consider an older women who has lived with DVA in her fifty years of marriage.

You might consider behaviours such as isolating a person from their family and friends, or monitoring their time and movements, or depriving them of their basic needs or access to support (health or social care). It can include threats to harm, kill, reveal personal and sensitive information (for example, threatening to 'out' somebody). It can include threats to children. This type of behaviour can be humiliating, as perpetrators may control where people eat, sleep, what they wear, where they go, who they talk to or how much money they have. It might include depriving a person of sleep, or forcing them to have sex, participate in demeaning or criminal activities. It can include daily 'put downs', arbitrary rules and dehumanising acts. Controlling and coercive behaviour can target aspects of a person's identity and circumstances such as age, ethnicity, asylum and immigration status, sexual orientation, gender, health or impairment. This list is only indicative and can include many more harmful and distressing abuses.

Messages for health and social care providers

Within the context of health and social care provision, tackling entrenched and systemic issues like DVA is never easy, particularly when targeting a marginalised group such as older people. However, age constitutes one of the protected characteristics of the Equality Act 2010, and so age discrimination should not occur in relation to access to health and social care for older women who are victims of DVA (EHRC, undated). Currently, however, by age 50 there is a considerable decrease in the number of victims/survivors accessing DVA services (NCALL, 2015). Much can be learnt from the evidence base as research suggests that under-reporting is commonplace with a significant number of reported cases that end up 'slipping through the cracks due to a lack of co-ordination among service providers' (NCALL, 2015: 8; Brandl et al., 2007). Therefore, a multi-agency response is essential in recognising older women as a subset of the larger group of victims/survivors as 'no one professional has all the expertise needed' (Brandl and Dawson, 2011: 320). The National Institute for Health and Care Excellence (NICE) also advocates a multi-agency strategy for tackling DVA, stating that:

> Domestic violence and abuse is a complex issue that needs sensitive handling by a range of health and social care professionals ... Working in a multi-agency partnership is the most effective way to approach the issue at both an operational and strategic level. (NICE, 2014: 6)

Typically, DVA services work on an empowerment model which advocates 'self-help'; however, this may be unfamiliar to older women and they may need more encouragement, reassurance and explicit guidance to make steps to leave an abusive relationship (LGA, 2015). On the other hand, once they learn that there are services to support them, older women may fully embrace the help on offer. In either case, person-centred assessments and care help to circumnavigate falling into the trap of misnaming abuse as elder abuse (if this is identified in the first place), and helps to avoid making judgements based on ageist stereotypes. Scott et al. (2004) identify a more significant problem as being the 'ideological gulf' between those working in DVA services and those providing care. This can happen, Scott et al. highlight, when DVA is treated as a sub-category of abuse against older people and therefore the specificity of older victims of DVA are not responded to. A practical example of how services may need to consider the particular needs of older victims/survivors is the requirement for facilities for those who have a disability or mobility problem and who may need specialist support or adaptations (Women's Aid, 2007).

Conclusion

This chapter has introduced the phenomenon of domestic violence and abuse (DVA) with a particular focus upon a hidden group of victims/survivors: older women. While it is difficult to get a sense of the extent of the problem, it is increasingly being recognised that within the context of older women's experiences of DVA there is 'a significant deficit in awareness and understanding within society as a whole and more particularly for those responsible for support and care provision' (Blood, 2004; McGarry et al., 2011: 3). As such, the difficulties with identification in terms of blurring the boundaries of DVA and elder abuse has been examined to alert the reader to the complexities of recognising DVA in later life within health and social care practice contexts. Moreover, the problem that older women do not always recognise their experiences of DVA is also acknowledged in relation to the obstacles to help-seeking behaviour. There are, however, many other barriers to asking for help and this should also be borne in mind. For example, the myth that DVA services and refuge accommodation are for younger women or those with children impacts on people's conception of eligibility and even validation in terms of acknowledging an older women's experiences as harmful as those for young mothers. This type of misperception may account for the lower uptake of services in women aged over 50 (NCALL, 2015).

This chapter may present a bleak picture in terms of the scale of the phenomenon and the challenges for service interventions. However, by exploring the barriers to help-seeking, some solutions are implicated. It is particularly helpful if practitioners are mindful of the gender-based nature of abuse as well as the particular dynamics of power and control which often constitute abusive behaviours. This enables practitioners to see beyond frailty and vulnerability as the reasons for one person's abuse of another and to see the more intricate weaving of power and control within intimate and familial relationships and to then see the impacts of these experiences. This is not to undermine the effects of elder abuse, but to distinguish the controlling and coercive aspects of DVA in combination with physical, sexual, emotional and financial abuse and the complexities when these present within the relationships with partners and significant others. Stark (2007) reminds us to analyse this in relation to the engrained structural problem of gender inequality. Lombard and Scott (2013) extend this analysis to argue that older women's experiences of DVA illuminate the intersection of sexism and ageism. It is useful, then, for practitioners to strive to locate their practice when supporting older victims/survivors of DVA at a micro-level (considering the therapeutic relationship between the practitioner and the service user) and within the context of macro-level influences and marginalisation of certain groups (older women). To conclude, this chapter has explored ideological and practical issues pertaining to older women's experiences of DVA and this discussion has highlighted several implications for health and social care providers, including ones connected to issues of identification, eligibility, accessibility, staff awareness and training, multi-disciplinary working models, policy and legal compliance.

Recommended reading

- LGA (2015) *Adult Safeguarding and Domestic Abuse: A Guide to Supporting Practitioners and Managers.* London: Local Government Association.

- NICE (2014) *Domestic Violence and Abuse: How Health Services, Social Care and the Organisations They Work With Can Respond Effectively.* London: National Institute for Health and Care Excellence.

- McGarry, J., Simpson, C. and Hinchliff-Smith, K. (2011) The impact of domestic abuse for older women: A review of the literature. *Health and Social Care in the Community*, 19(1): 3–14.

Relevant web links

- www.womensaid.org.uk **Women's Aid** is a grassroots federation working together to provide life-saving services and build a future where domestic violence is not tolerated.

- www.equalityhumanrights.com **The Equality and Human Rights Commission** states 'we live in a country with a long history of upholding people's rights, valuing diversity and challenging intolerance. The EHRC seeks to maintain and strengthen this heritage while identifying and tackling areas where there is still unfair discrimination or where human rights are not being respected'.

- http://elderabuse.org.uk **Action on Elder Abuse** is the only UK charity working to protect and prevent the abuse of vulnerable older adults.

References

Action on Elder Abuse (2015) *What is Elder Abuse?* Available from: http://elderabuse.org.uk/what-is-elder-abuse/ (accessed 12 March 2016).

Beaulaurier, R., Self, L. and Newman, F. (2008) Barriers to help seeking for older women who experienced intimate partner violence: a descriptive model. *Journal of Women and Aging*, 20: 231–248.

Blood, I. (2004) *Older Women and Domestic Violence*. Available from: www.ageuk.org.uk/documents/en-gb/for-professionals/communities-and-inclusion/id2382_2_older_women_and_domestic_violence_summary_2004_pro.pdf?dtrk=true (accessed 12 March 2016).

Brandl, B. and Dawson, L. (2011) Responding to victims of abuse in later life in the United States. *The Journal of Adult Protection,* 13(6): 315–322.

Brandl, B., Dyer, C.B., Heisler, C.J., Stiegel, A. and Thomas, R.W. (eds) (2007) *Elder Abuse Detection and Intervention: A Collaborative Approach*. New York: Springer.

Donovan, C. and Hester, M. (2014) *Domestic Violence and Sexuality: What's Love Got to Do with it?* Bristol: Policy Press.

EHRC (undated) *Age Discrimination*. Available from: www.equalityhumanrights.com/your-rights/equal-rights/age-discrimination (accessed 12 March 2016).

Goergen, T. (2011) Older women and domestic violence. *Journal of Adult Protection,* 13(6). DOI: http://dx.doi.org.salford.idm.oclc.org/10.1108/jap.2011.54913faa.001.

Groves, N. and Thomas, T. (2014) *Domestic Violence and Criminal Justice*. Abingdon: Routledge.

Guy, J., Feinstein, L. and Griffiths, A. (2014) *Early Intervention in Domestic Violence and Abuse.* London: Early Intervention Foundation.

Hightower, J. (2002) *Violence and abuse in the lives of older women: is it elder abuse or violence against women: Does it make any difference?* Background paper for INSTRAW Electronic Discussion Forum Gender Aspects of Violence and Abuse of Older Persons, 15–26.

HM Government (2013) *Ready for Ageing. Select Committee on Public Service and Demographic Change – First Report.* Available from: www.publications.parliament.uk/pa/ld201213/ldselect/ldpublic/140/14002.htm (accessed 13 March 2016).

Home Office (2013) *Domestic Violence and Abuse.* Available at: www.gov.uk/government/publications/definition-of-domestic-violence-and-abuse-guide-for-local-areas (accessed 13 January 2016).

_____(2015) *Controlling or Coercive Behaviour in an Intimate or Family Relationship: Statutory Guidance Framework.* London: Home Office.

Kelly, J.B. and Johnson, M. (2008) Differentiation among types of intimate partner violence: research update and implications for interventions. *Family Court Review,* 46(3): 476–499.

LGA (2015) *Adult safeguarding and domestic abuse: a guide to support practitioners and managers.* London: Local Government Association.

Lombard, N. and McMillan, L. (2013) *Violence Against Women: Current Theory and Practice in Domestic Abuse, Sexual Violence and Exploitation.* London: Jessica Kingsley Publishers.

Lombard, N. and Scott, M. (2013) Domestic abuse and older women: where ageism and sexism intersect. In N. Lombard and L. McMillan *Violence Against Women: Current Theory and Practice in Domestic Abuse, Sexual Violence and Exploitation.* London: Jessica Kingsley Publishers.

McGarry, J., Simpson, C. and Hinchliff-Smith, K. (2011) The impact of domestic abuse for older women: a review of the literature. *Health and Social Care in the Community,* 19(1): 3–14.

Mowlam, A., Tennant, R., Dixon, J. and McCreadie, C. (2007) *UK Study of Abuse and Neglect of Older People: Qualitative Findings.* London: National Centre for Social Research.

NCALL (2015) *Special Collection: Preventing and responding to Domestic and Sexual Violence in Later Life.* Minnesota: NCALL.

NICE (2014) *Domestic Violence and Abuse: How Health Services, Social Care and the Organisations They Work with Can Respond Effectively.* London: NICE.

O'Keefe, M., Hills., A. and Doyle, M. et al. (2007) *UK Study of Abuse and Neglect of Older People.* London: Department of Health.

ONS (2015a) *User Guide to Crime Statistics for England and Wales.* London: ONS.

_____ (2015b) *Chapter 4: Violent Crime and Sexual Offences – Intimate Personal Violence and Serious Sexual Assault.* Available from: www.ons.gov.uk/peoplepopulationand community/crimeandjustice/compendium/focusonviolentcrimeandsexualoffences/2015-02-12/chapter4violentcrimeandsexualoffencesintimatepersonalviolenceand serioussexualassault#prevalence-of-intimate-violence-extent (accessed 13 March 2016).

Scott, M., McKie, L., Morton, S., Seddon., E. and Wosoff, F. (2004) *Older Women and Domestic Violence in Scotland: '… and for 39 years I got on with it'.* Edinburgh: Health Scotland.

Stark, E. (2007) *Coercive Control: How Men Entrap Women in Personal Life.* New York: Oxford University Press.

Turner, A., Spangler, D. and Brandl, B. (2010) Domestic abuse in later life. In L.L. Lockhart and F.S. Danis (eds) *Domestic Violence: Intersectionality and Culturally Competence Practice.* New York: Columbia University Press.

UN (2002) *World Population Ageing: 1950–2050.* Available from: www.un.org/esa/population/publications/worldageing19502050/ (accessed 13 March 2016).

Weeks, L.E. and LeBlanc, K. (2011) An ecological synthesis of research on older women's experiences of intimate partner violence. *Journal of Women and Aging,* 23(4): 283–304.

World Health Organization (WHO)/INPEA (2002) *Missing Voices: Views of Older Persons on Elder Abuse.* Available from: www.who.int/ageing/projects/elder_abuse/missing_voices/en/ (accessed 13 March 2016).

Wolf, R. (2000) The nature and scope of elder abuse. *Generations – Journal of the American Society on Aging.* 24(2): 6–12.

Women's Aid (2007) *Older Women and Domestic Violence: An Overview.* Available from: www.womensaid.org.uk/domestic-violence-articles.asp?section=000100010 02200110002&itemid=920 (accessed 14 October 2015).

Zink, T., Jacobson, C., Regan. S., Fisher, B. and Pabst, S. (2004) Hidden victims: the healthcare needs and experiences of older women in abusive relationships. *Journal of Women's Health,* 13(8): 898–908.

CONCLUSION

Anya Ahmed and Michaela Rogers

Through its focus on professional practice, an overarching aim of this book was to encourage students as present and future practitioners to question essentialist notions of difference and to consider how marginalisation, social exclusion and inequality operate. We highlighted cross-disciplinary themes within the context of current debates across health and social care education and practice, and at the core of the discussion we premised that 'good practice' in health and social care should be anti-oppressive and inclusive practice underpinned by the relevant legislative and policy frameworks. Moreover, the book has shown how, in certain cases, 'good practice' should go beyond legislative and policy frameworks as these can be understood as 'not going far enough' in terms of addressing inequality and exclusion.

In the preceding chapters we addressed the theoretical, legal and policy frameworks which shape the contexts in which diversity and exclusion are understood and addressed. Through focusing on a range of diverse 'groups' in society, we highlighted some important considerations for health and social care professionals in terms of the ways that difference can be experienced, and how processes of exclusion and marginalisation operate. The Equality Act (EA) 2010, as well as health and social care professional standards of ethics and conduct, state that people should not receive less favourable treatment due to background or individual characteristics, and that discrimination should be challenged and addressed. However, as the contributors have explained by highlighting the experiences of young people, trans people, Roma, Deaf people, people with autism spectrum disorder, people from BME backgrounds with dementia and older women experiencing domestic violence or abuse, there are numerous barriers to accessing services, and these barriers also reflect and compound discriminatory social processes leading to exclusion and marginalisation. In this concluding chapter, we bring together cross-disciplinary themes and provide an overview of the processes and outcomes of exclusion experienced by the identified groups. We also highlight the implications for health and social care practice and provide a summary of our key messages of the book. First though, consider the following:

Reflection

After reading the discussions throughout the book, what common experiences do the 'groups' share at societal level and how are these experiences reproduced in relation to

---

their experiences of health and social care services? Can you identify any significant differences between the groups? Can you identify any differences within groups?

In the introductory chapter we presented the legal, policy, practice and theoretical backgrounds framing the issues discussed throughout the book and clarified our use of concepts and terminology. In doing so, we highlighted the need to explore not only the characteristics of each of the groups under discussion but also the processes and structures impacting on each group or individual's experiences of the world because, as Thompson (2012) notes, difference and diversity are the roots of discrimination.

We demonstrated that notions of diversity and equality are not straightforward, however, and, in categorical terms, are certainly not limited to the protected characteristics offered within the Equality Act 2010. We problematised the notions of social exclusion/inclusion showing that the dimensions of each are not discrete but imbued with overlaps and synergies. In this sense, one can experience the world in many different ways as either included and as a member of the dominant majority (for example, as a heterosexual man) but also as excluded and as occupying a minority position (if, for example, that individual was also from a Roma background). We end this chapter by setting out a discussion of the practice and policy frameworks which underpin inclusive and anti-oppressive practice. This indicates to the reader the ways in which everyday practice can counter the impacts of marginalisation, discrimination and exclusion.

In Chapter 2, Morton and Myers highlighted that health and social care services have become increasingly aware of diversity and the need for inclusive practice, and that changes in practice and the way that services are delivered have also had unintended consequences for service users. For example, although emphasising difference is a key feature of anti-discriminatory practice, practice can reinforce exclusion by an over-emphasis of difference. Morton and Myers also questioned whether the term 'culture' is useful to understand difference in health and social care and concluded that it obscured power differences between 'dominant' cultures and other cultures. They argued that a more helpful approach would involve practitioners adopting a reflexive approach to understanding difference and therefore to problematise essentialist notions of diversity while acknowledging the context in which difference is constructed. This, they maintain, is important since non-reflexive practice runs the risk of services reinforcing discrimination and the marginalisation of service users.

In Chapter 3, McAndrew and Warne explained that mental illness disproportionately affects young people, and that the psychological well-being of young people who use mental health services and those who have taken on caring roles is of particular concern for health and social care agendas. They suggested that young people with mental health issues are not properly taken into account in the design and delivery of services, and that they also experience barriers accessing such services. McAndrew and Warne highlight that although good practice guidance exists, there is a need to go further: they make recommendations with regard to how inclusive practice in health and social care can better meet the needs of young people including importance of involving young people in research, evaluating services and in the design of professional education.

In Chapter 4, Brammer, Kennedy and Binns explained that children and young people with autism spectrum disorders experience challenges regarding social interactions with people and the environment, and that such challenges are brought into sharp focus when there is a need for a healthcare intervention. They suggest that the experiences of health systems can be improved through collaborative working and making reasonable adjustments to promote access and inclusion, and emphasise that there is a need for increased awareness of autism at society level, reinforcing the notion that inequalities experienced at organisational level reflect wider inequalities in society.

In Chapter 5, Scullion and Brown identify Roma as one of the most socially excluded communities in Europe and highlight a range of structural and cultural barriers which affect the health outcomes, educational attainment, employment, housing and social welfare experiences of this group. They explain that although policy and practice have addressed the exclusion of Roma at a European and national level, many initiatives do not offer long-term solutions. They suggest that future approaches to Roma inclusion need to ensure the involvement of Roma in their development and implementation. This echoes the suggestions put forward by McAndrew and Warne, who also argue that inclusivity in services is contingent on involving marginalised groups in the design and delivery of services.

In Chapter 6, Rogers explains that trans people are becoming increasingly visible in social life, and as such visibility increases, so too do the social problems that affect them. She argues that there are multiple barriers for trans people accessing health and social care services and puts forward a conceptual framework to facilitate an understanding of experiences of social exclusion and marginalisation. Rogers highlights that legal protection for this marginalised group centres on trans people identifying with a limited gender binary framework and demonstrates the exclusionary processes in operation for people who do not ascribe to normative social categories.

In Chapter 7, Hough and Sharples explain that Deaf people have experienced degrees of exclusion from the mainstream of society for millennia, and that such exclusion creates challenges for them, their family relationships and their ability to access health and social care services. They suggest that working towards inclusion supports better education, employment and healthy lives.

In Chapter 8, Ahmed, Egal and Mohammed explain that dementia has been identified as the biggest health and social care challenge facing society due largely to an ageing population. They argue that the National Dementia Strategy emphasises that health and social care service providers should take account of BME dementia needs, yet the needs of these communities are not being met. Moreover, they argue that little is known in terms of the needs of BME people with dementia and end the chapter by offering a number of ways in which this can be addressed.

In Chapter 9, Rogers suggests that the term domestic violence and abuse (DVA) is an appropriate term to refer to the gender-based nature of violence and abuse in older women's intimate and family relationships, since it more accurately captures the gendered experience than the term 'elder abuse'. This type of understanding helps practitioners to see beyond age, and perhaps frailty and vulnerability, to identify the specific controlling, and often gendered, dynamics of DVA. She explains that the DVA experiences of older women are often hidden and that there are particular barriers to help-seeking behaviour for women in this age group. Rogers argues that a multi-agency response is critical to helping older women leave abusive relationships and move towards recovery with appropriate support.

It is clear, then, that adopting a non-essentialist approach when working with diverse (and heterogeneous) groups is key to inclusive practice, and such lessons can be applied to the different populations under discussion here. For example, individuals and groups can be stigmatised and marginalised *as a result of* inhabiting the categories of young service user/carer, trans, Deaf, autistic, BME, Roma and so on. This can lead to exclusion on a macro level and also to inequity in experiences of health and social care services. This leads to poorer outcomes, and again this compounds and reinforces marginalisation. In spite of having protection under law and policy, and through professional codes of practice, Deaf people, people with autism spectrum disorder, trans people, Roma, young service users, those with mental health problems, older women and older people from BME backgrounds experience inequality in health and social care services. Further, austerity measures and cuts to welfare funding pose additional difficulties for health and social care providers with resources becoming increasingly scarce.

INDEX

Abuse
  Physical 38, 134–147
  Sexual 38, 134–147
Access 8, 9
Aging 8, 122–123, 124
  Population 120, 122–123
Allied health professions 11, 26–28
Alzheimer's disease 124
Anti-discriminatory practice, see Anti-
  oppressive practice
Anti-oppressive practice 7, 11–12, 26,
  27– 28, 52
Ascription 10
Asperger's Syndrome 57
Assessment 30–32
Attitudes 52, 57
Autism Act 2009 55, 58
Autism spectrum disorders 52–64, 153
  Comorbidities 54

Black and Minority Ethnic (BME) popula-
  tion 6, 120–123, 126
Black Feminism 10
Bureaucracy 59

CAMHS 41
Carers 54, 129–130
  Barriers to services 126
  Needs assessment 125–126
  Social movement 40–42
Census 123, 130
Citizenship
Clinical Commissioning Groups 125
Coercive control 137, 144–145
Communication 42–43, 54, 57–59, 63
  Barriers 57
  Listening 41, 43, 59
Communities 10, 11–12, 27

Consent 44
Cultural competence 25–34, 152
Cultural deficit 32
Culture 11, 22–34, 121–122, 129, 131
  Asian 23

Darwin 122
Deaf, deaf definition 105
  Access to services 109–117
  Children 109
  Communication 113–116
  Deaf gene 107
  Disability 106–107
  Disability Discrimination Act
    1995 109
  Disability Rights Movement 108
  Education 109
  Employment 116
  Healthcare 110–111
  Human Rights Act 1998 116–117
  Medical model 106, 107
  Psychiatric services 111–113
  Social model 106, 107
  Social exclusion 105–106, 114–115,
    153
Decision-making 130
Dementia 120–131, 154
  Annual spending 125–127
  Definition 123
  Dementia Care Pathway 124, 125
  Health inequalities 121
  Needs assessment 125–126, 138
Department of Health 121
Depression 38
Disability 6
Discourse 27–28, 33–34, 43
Discrimination 8, 11–12, 15–18, 55
Diversity and difference 6–8, 22–24, 122

Domestic violence and abuse 31–32, 38, 134–147, 154
  Age discrimination 145
  Ageing population 135
  Analysis of experience 137–139
  Barriers to seeking help 141–143, 147
  Definitions 135–137, 144
  Disability 139
  Dynamics in later life 139–140
  Elder abuse 134, 135
  Enablers for help seeking 143, 147
  Forms of abuse 136, 137
  Legal framwork 144–145
  Measuring prevalence 137–139
  Messages for health and social care providers 145–145, 147
  NICE strategy 146

Education 38–40
Employment 6, 9
Empowerment 24, 26, 41, 43, 146
End of life care 30
Environment 59, 61, 63
Epistemic reflexivity 28–29
Equality 6–8
Equality Act 2010 7, 8, 13–17, 55, 58, 93, 108, 125, 145, 151
Equality and Human Rights Commission 13
Equality Duty, see Public Sector Equality Duty
Equal opportunities 8
Essentialism 22–24
Ethical symmetry 43
Ethics 8, 55
Ethnic minority, see Black and Minority Ethnic (BME) population
Ethnicity 8, 12, 14–18, 22–23, 31–32, 121–122
European Convention on Human Rights 13–14
European Court of Human Rights 13–14
Evidence-base 12, 60, 121

Feminist Literature 87

Gender 6, 12, 22, 38, 39, 53, 87, 88
  Cisgender 86, 87, 89–91, 99, 100
Gender binary 88, 89, 90, 92, 100
Gender dysphoria 89, 94
Gender identity 93
Gender inequality 137, 147
Gender norm 86, 87, 98, 99, 100
Gender spectrum 89
  Andogyne 89
  Cross dresser 89
  Gender queer 89
Gender reassignment 95
Gender outlaws 93
Gender Recognition Act 2004 93, 94, 95
Gender transgression 93
GPs, see Practitioners
Groups, see Communities

Harassment 15–16
Health
  Barriers to healthcare 39–40, 56–59
  BME dementia needs 121
  Checks 59
  Needs assessment 60, 63
  Passport 58
Health and Social Care Act 2012 55, 58
Health Care and Professions Council 8
Heterosexism and heteronormativity 23–24
Homophobia 13, 24
Hospital 60–63
Human rights 13–14, 16
Human Rights Act 1998 13–14

Identity 10, 22–34, 122
Inclusive practice model 7
Inequality 6, 11
  Health related 53–54
Intersectionality 6–7, 10

Labelling 54
Labour market 9, 122–123

Language 11, 43–44, 53, 122,
   127–128
Learning disability 17, 52–53, 58–59
LGBT 13, 24

Macro, *see* Structural Factors
Marginalisation 10, 12, 22, 47, 130
Member states (of the EU) 14
Memory clinic 128
Mental health 38–47, 55–56, 127
Mentor 45
Migration 120, 122–123
Minority ethnic, *see* Black and Minority
   Ethnic (BME) population
Modernisation 40

National Dementia Strategy 12, 121,
   125–126, 131
National Health Service (NHS) 55, 60, 125
National Institute for Health and Care
   Excellence (NICE) 125
National Service Framework for Autism
   2003 54
New Labour 9

Oppression 11–12
Othering 22, 30

Participation 42–45
   Barriers 9
   In research 40, 43–44
   Young people 42–44
Payments for participation in
   research 45
PCS model 11–12
Personal level 11
Person-centred approaches 60
Pervasive Developmental Disorder 52
Practice Wisdom 12
Practitioners 12–13, 121
   GPs 127, 130–1
   Healthcare 7, 5–6, 59
   Nurse specialist 59
   Physicians/clinicians 55, 57
   Social care 7

Primary care 127
Positionality 10
Poverty 6, 9, 10, 56
Power 9, 12, 14, 23, 28, 40
Privilege 12
Professional bodies 8
Professional codes 8
Protected characteristics 8, 15–16
Public Sector Equality Duty 16–18

Queer literature 87

Race 23–26, 31–32, 121–122
Racism 23, 25, 33
Radiology 57–58, 60–63
Reasonable adjustments 55,
   57–60, 63
Reflective practice 27–28
Reflexivity 27–29, 30–31, 33–34,
   152
Refugees 56
Religion 14, 16, 127, 129
Reminiscence work 128
Research 42–45
Residential care homes 129
Resource distribution 53, 55, 60
Risk factors 54–55, 126
Roma and travellers 56, 153
Roma
   Children 75
   Definitions 70–71
   Education 74–75
   Employment 75
   European context 72–77
   Health 73–74
   Housing 73
   Inclusion (football as a tool) 79–80
   Policy and practice 78–79
   Social exclusion 72–77
   UK context 77–78

Screening and diagnostic tools 54–55,
   57–58, 128
Service users 40–42
Sex 87, 88

Sexuality   12–13, 16, 17, 24–25, 29–31, 87, 88
  Asexuality   88
  Bisexuality   88
  Heteronormativity   86, 87, 90, 98, 99, 100
  Pansexuality   88
Social exclusion   9–10, 123, 130
Social inclusion   9–10
Social Service Departments   125
Social work   8, 11, 28, 46
  Assessment   30–32
Standards of Conduct, Performance & Ethics   8
Stigma   39, 47, 121, 126–127
Structural factors   7, 10, 12, 33

Tokenism   42
Training   59, 63
Trans
  Barriers to accessing services   96–99
  Citizenship   92–95
  Embodiment   98
  Equality Act 2010   89, 94, 95
  Equality   99
  Female to male   89
  Gender   88
  Gender queer   89
  Health   99
  Inclusion   99
  Inequality   86, 87
  Intersex   88
  Male to female   89
  Marginalisation   86, 87, 91, 92
  Media   93
  Misgendering   97
  Passing   91

Policy framework   94–96
Practice issues   89
Queer   96–100
Self-identification   97
Sex   88
Social exclusion   91–92, 153
Subjectivity   91
Stigma   87
Structural oppression   90–91
Underresesearched   91
Transitioning   86
Transgender   92
Transidentity   89
Transphobia   96
Transpractice   88
Transsexuality   89
Transitions   89
  To adult services   62–63

Underrepresentation   121
Unemployment   6

Vascular dementia   124
Victimisation   15–16

White populations   32–33, 122
Winterbourne View Hospital   55
Women   6, 22
Women and Equalities Committee Enquiry   93, 95, 96
World Health Organisation   123

Young carers   39–40, 46–47, 153
Young people
  Depression   38
  Mental health   38–39, 41–42, 153
  Stress   53